BREAK THROUGH

20 Surprising Ways
to Unleash Heaven's Resources

DAVID CERULLO

BREAK
THROUGH

20 Surprising Ways
to Unleash Heaven's Resources

by David Cerullo

Copyright © 2014 by David Cerullo, Inspiration Ministries

ISBN: 978-1-936177-23-3

Published by:

INSPIRATION MINISTRIES
PO Box 7750
Charlotte, NC 28241
+1 803-578-1899
inspiration.org

Printed in the United States of America.

DEDICATION

In grateful appreciation to
our faithful Inspiration Partners...

Your prayers and financial seeds are
changing countless lives around the world
—both in this life and for all eternity.

Your reward in Heaven will be great!

CONTENTS

One prayer can accomplish more
than a thousand plans.

MARK BATTERSON

Prepare for Your Breakthrough

Precious friend, when you combine the promises of God's Word with a passion to seek Him in prayer…**MIRACLES HAPPEN!** Heaven's amazing resources are released into your life. Instead of living in the Land of Never Enough, or Barely Enough, you are finally able to experience the Land of MORE than Enough.

But this kind of life begins with *gratitude*, as you recognize how much your Heavenly Father loves you, and as you acknowledge what He has already done for you in Christ.

Every single one of us has been blessed immeasurably by God. If He had only done one thing for you and me today, and that one thing was to send His Son Jesus to die on the Cross to pay the penalty for our sins, wouldn't that have been enough? If Jesus just redeemed us from the law of sin and death, giving us the great hope of eternal life with Him in Heaven, wouldn't that have been enough?

Of course it would be! He paid a debt He did not owe. He took our place on the Cross. The penalty of death was *our* sentence, but He paid our debt in full. Hallelujah! Thank you, Jesus!

Because of the power of sin and the resulting curse it brought, this world is impacted with pain, suffering, sickness, sorrow, addiction, poverty, and every form of death. These are things God never intended for us to experience. Instead, Jesus stated God's will for us in John 10:10: *"I have come that they may have life, and that they may have it more abundantly."*

The apostle gives a glimpse of what this abundant life means: *"He who did not spare His own Son, but delivered Him up for us all, how shall He not with Him also freely give us all things?"* (Romans 8:32) You see, God already has given us His Son. And because of that amazing demonstration of unmerited love, we can trust Him to *"freely give us ALL things"*!

WHAT BREAKTHROUGH DO YOU NEED?

Despite the great work God has already done for us in Christ, we all have various kinds of needs. To be candid, we all are broken people in many different ways. But the good news is that Jesus came to set us free from the penalty and power of sin. The curse has been cancelled for those who embrace the Cross (Galatians 3:13).

I don't know what your brokenness may be today. Nor do I know the breakthrough you're crying out for as you read this book. But I do know what the Bible promises in Mark 10:27:

"WITH GOD ALL THINGS ARE POSSIBLE!"

Through the power of prayer, you can transform your world, and overcome problems that have plagued you for years. You also can release God's miracles in the lives of your friends and loved ones, and you can join with other believers in seeking revival in your church and your nation.

Dear one, let's be honest: In order to get your breakthrough, you may have to add **PATIENCE** and **PERSISTENCE** to your faith (Hebrews 6:12). The answer you seek may take some time, and you may have to *battle* for your *breakthrough:*

- Like the widow who continually petitioned the unjust judge, you must pray until your breakthrough comes (Luke 18:1-8).
- Just as Jacob was willing to wrestle with God all night until the blessing came, you will need to hang on to God's promises with steadfast faith (Genesis 32:24-30).

- Even though you see only scant evidence on the horizon, you must proclaim that your victory is at hand (1 Kings 18:41-45).

When you're willing to exhibit this kind of determined, radical faith, you can expect explosive results. No matter what need you or your loved ones may be facing today, I encourage you to obey God and then believe His promises as you pray. When you have done your part, stand in faith and *never give up*. As Jesus encouraged us in Matthew 7:7:

"Keep asking...keep seeking...and keep knocking!"

Barbara and I are joining our prayers with yours today. We're asking God to draw you into a place of greater intimacy with Him, so He can give you fantastic blessings and breakthroughs on your journey of faith.

God bless you!

David

Only one life, 'twill soon be past,
Only what's done for Christ will last.

C.T. STUDD

1 RESPOND TO HISTORY'S BIGGEST BREAKTHROUGH

There are two sides of every supernatural event: the *"super"* (something only God can do) and the *"natural"* (something He expects us to do). This principle is found throughout the Bible. For example, when we give God our seeds, He gives us His harvests. When we release our earthly resources, God gives us His heavenly resources.

God has repeatedly demonstrated His ability to take a common shepherd's staff and infuse it with miracle-working power…defeat 1,000 Philistines with the jawbone of a donkey…and turn five loaves and a few fish into a meal for thousands of people. When we obediently give Him our *"natural,"* He gladly supplies us with His *"super."*

That's why supernatural breakthroughs nearly always involve two distinct parts: God's part and our part. And before we move on to a discussion of how to receive a breakthrough of Heaven's resources, we first need to understand the *biggest breakthrough in all of human history:* God's love breaking through every barrier to rescue lost humanity.

For over 1,000 years, God's presence was mostly experienced just once a year, when the high priest entered the Holy of Holies in the tabernacle and then the temple. The Lord's radiant glory was shielded from view by a thick veil separating the Holy place from the Holy of Holies.

Historians say this massive veil was 60 feet long, 30 feet wide, and four inches thick. It was so heavy that 300 priests were needed to lift it, and it was so strong that even a team of horses would have been unable to pull it apart.

Yet something amazing happened when Jesus died for us on Cross: *"Jesus cried out with a loud voice, and breathed His last. Then the veil of the temple was torn in two from top to bottom"* (Mark 15:37-38). The thick curtain that no one on earth could have torn was torn by God Himself—*"from top to bottom"!*

Do you see how significant this was?

When Jesus died for us, God's LOVE broke through!

It was *love* that motivated God to send His only Son to earth in the first place (John 3:16), and that same *love* was on full display when Christ died for us, even while we were still sinners (Romans 5:8).

At Jesus' birth and then again at the Cross, God broke through to us. And Jesus' Resurrection three days later proved He was ALIVE forever as our Savior, Lord, and Advocate.

But then notice the POWER released when God's love ripped the temple veil in two, just so lost humanity could come to Him unimpeded. What a dramatic statement that His love would no longer remain behind any veils or religious rituals.

Friend, take a moment to let this amazing breakthrough from God sink in. *Nothing* is hindering you from coming boldly to God's throne of grace to receive what you need from Him today (Hebrews 4:16). You can draw near to Him and receive whatever heavenly resources you need for a life of victory.

BREAKING THROUGH TO *HIM*

So, what is your role in this supernatural exchange? In decisive, dramatic fashion, God has broken through every obstacle to open wide the doors of Heaven to you. Yet in order to receive your breakthrough, you may need to "break through" some daunting circumstances as well. As God has done so much to break through to YOU, you may need to also take some steps to break through to HIM.

One day Jesus was teaching in someone's home in Capernaum. News had spread, and there was a packed house: *"Soon the house where he was staying was so packed with visitors that there was no more room, even outside the door"* (Mark 2:2). About that time, four men arrived late to the meeting. They needed a miracle—not for themselves, but for a paralyzed friend they were carrying on a mat.

However, there was a problem, and it seemed insurmountable. The crowd was so great, it looked impossible to get the paralyzed man to Jesus. Most of us would have given up at that point. After all, they had done their best. And they already had carried the man a long distance.

> *You can draw near to Him and receive whatever heavenly resources you need for a life of victory.*

But these men didn't quit. Devising a very creative solution, they climbed on the rooftop and dug a hole through the roof above where Jesus was sitting. Then they found a way to lower the man on his mat, right in front of the Lord!

The people listening to Jesus' message were probably quite annoyed at this rude interruption. And I'm sure the man who owned the house wasn't happy about the hole dug in his roof!

But we're told that Jesus SAW their faith, and He took notice (v. 5). I love that, don't you? While people sometimes speak of "faith" as if it's some kind of nebulous and intangible force, this story illustrates that true faith is something you can SEE! And make no mistake about it: When we take a step of faith and obedience, the Lord always notices.

Consider your life today. Do you have an active, dynamic, obedient faith, like these four men displayed? Is your faith audacious enough to dig a hole in someone's roof in order to bring a friend to Jesus?

Because of these men's faith and their willing to dig past every obstacle in their way, their friend's life was radically transformed. First, Jesus forgave his sins. Then He told the paralyzed man, *"Stand up, pick up your mat, and go home!"* (v. 11)

People were amazed when the man *"jumped up, grabbed his mat, and walked through the stunned onlookers"* (v. 12). But this miraculous outcome occurred because four men took a bold step of faith to bring their paralyzed friend to the Savior.

ARE YOU READY TO BREAK THROUGH?

Most of us need some kind of breakthrough today, whether in our own life or the life of a friend or loved one. The paralyzed man needed a physical healing, but you probably know someone who needs God to intervene in their marriage, their children, their emotions, or their finances. And I'm sure you also know someone who needs to be brought to the feet of Jesus in order to receive His life-changing salvation.

Whatever the need may be, I encourage you to pause and ask God for His instructions today. Is there a friend who needs your help? Is there a "roof" you must dig through? Is there a seed you need to sow?

You see, in order to unleash the resources and blessings of Heaven, we need to respond to the breakthrough of God's love for us in Christ. Love sent Jesus from Heaven to earth and then to the agony of the Cross. He broke through the temple veil and every barrier our sin had erected.

We should respond to His love by passionately breaking through every barrier that keeps us on the outer courts!

It broke Jesus' heart when the believers in Ephesus drifted away from Him and left their *"first love"* (Revelation 2:1-4). After He had done so much to break through human sinfulness, pride, and apathy, how could they become so distracted by religious activities and the cares of the world that they lost their intimacy with Him?

Later we see Jesus knocking on the door of the church at Laodicea (Revelation 3:14-20). No longer would He rip apart a thick curtain or break through closed doors. Instead, He knocks. He waits. He speaks tenderly, inviting us to hear His loving words and open the door to Him.

Friend, I pray His awesome love will break through to you today, penetrating every barrier and obstacle. May you hear His loving invitation and open your heart wide to Him. The King of Kings wants to come and dine with you!

You were made by God and for God,
and until you understand that,
life will never make sense.

RICK WARREN

2 BREAK THROUGH TO A NEW SEASON OF BLESSINGS

There are only two kinds of people: those who need a breakthrough now, and those who will need one soon. No one is exempt. As Jesus told us, the sun and rain are experienced by both the righteous and the unrighteous (Matthew 5:45).

The pages of Scripture are filled with examples of people who received amazing turnarounds from God. The Lord provides us with these wonderful stories to encourage us by His faithful intervention in the lives of His people, as Paul tells us in Romans 15:4:

> *Whatever was written in earlier times was written for our instruction, so that through perseverance and the encouragement of the Scriptures we might have hope.*

God wants to step into the circumstances of your life today! As you call upon Him in prayer, He will break through the dark and stormy clouds to touch you at the point of your need. He will replace your parched ground with abundance, and your winter season with the fragrance of spring.

Even as children of God, each of us will face a "winter season" at one time or another. This could be a divorce, an illness, the loss of a loved one, a financial setback, or struggles with our children. When a difficult situation brings *winter* into our life, it's easy to feel frustrated, stressed-out, depressed, or overwhelmed.

Even those who have already experienced the *ultimate* new beginning —the new birth in Jesus Christ (John 3:7)—will periodically find themselves in a difficult spot. Despite being faithful to the Lord, every believer will, from time to time, need a fresh start...a release from their winter season.

The good news is that a breakthrough of God's love and favor is available to anyone who truly wants one. It's not a matter of wishful thinking or just trying harder, and we don't have to be in any doubt about where to find such a breakthrough. Revelation 21:5 tells us: *"He who sits on the throne said, 'Behold, I am making **ALL things new.**'"*

THE SOURCE OF YOUR HELP

Perhaps you've been looking for answers to life's questions in all the wrong places: unhealthy friendships, addictions, immorality, binging on food, pornography, or material gain. These may have temporarily distracted you from the real issue, but instead of fixing the ache in your heart, it only grew worse.

However, if you need a turnaround of some kind today, you can be *certain* where to find it: at the throne of Jesus, the One who is able to make ALL things new!

The psalmist understood this principle well: *"My help comes from the LORD, Who made heaven and earth"* (Psalm 121:2). In his day, as in ours, many people were looking to other sources for their comfort, security, or breakthrough. Some were seeking help from other gods, while others were trusting in their own strength.

> *If you need a turnaround today, you can find it at the throne of Jesus, the One who is able to make ALL things new.*

Why did the psalmist choose to put his trust in God instead of other sources? Because he recognized the Lord as the One *"Who made heaven and earth."* If God is the Creator of the entire universe, surely He is powerful enough to transform our circumstances and give us breakthroughs today.

Pause for a moment and ask yourself: Where are you looking for your breakthrough? If you find that you've been looking to sources other than the Lord, ask Him to forgive you. Remember this testimony from another psalmist: *"As the eyes of servants look to the hand of their masters…so our eyes look to the LORD our God, until He has mercy on us"* (Psalm 123:2).

A SOLUTION FOR ALL SEASONS

No matter what season of life you may find yourself in today, the same solution applies. Make sure you are *"looking unto Jesus, the author and finisher of our faith"* (Hebrews 12:2). Even if you've been tripped up by life's circumstances, He will lift you up:

> *The LORD helps the fallen*
> *and lifts those bent beneath their loads.*
>
> *The eyes of all look to you in hope;*
> *you give them their food as they need it.*
>
> *When you open your hand,*
> *you satisfy the hunger and thirst of every living thing*
> (Psalm 145:14-16 NLT).

The Message offers uplifting paraphrases of verse 14: *"GOD gives a hand to those down on their luck, gives a fresh start to those ready to quit."* So if you've felt *"ready to quit,"* remember that God can quickly reverse your circumstances through His amazing favor.

God is a faithful God in *every* season. His mercies are new every morning (Lamentations 3:21-23). He will NEVER leave you, no matter how difficult the circumstances may seem (Hebrews 13:5).

God can turn your barren winters into fruitful springs…times of drought into abundant harvests (Genesis 26:1-14). Those who trust in Him never need to worry about the changing seasons:

Blessed are those who trust in the LORD
    and have made the LORD their hope and confidence.

They are like trees planted along a riverbank,
    with roots that reach deep into the water.

Such trees are not bothered by the heat
    or worried by long months of drought.

Their leaves stay green,
    and they never stop producing fruit
(Jeremiah 17:7-8 NLT).

What an encouraging picture of the kind of life we can have when our roots reach deeply into the soil of God's love. Like the woman described in Proverbs 31, we will be able to "smile at the future," confident God is preparing blessings and breakthroughs for us in the days ahead (Proverbs 31:25 NASB).

A GLIMPSE OF SPRINGTIME

If you're going through a winter season in your marriage, your job, your health, your finances, your emotions, or your children, God wants to give you confident HOPE that a better season is ahead. However, you may find yourself doubting that you'll ever see springtime again. And perhaps it's hard even to picture what an abundant life could look like.

If so, take a look at this beautiful description of springtime through the eyes of King Solomon:

Look around you: Winter is over;
    the winter rains are over, gone!

Spring flowers are in blossom all over.
    The whole world's a choir—and singing!

Spring warblers are filling the forest
    with sweet arpeggios.

> *Lilacs are exuberantly purple and perfumed,*
> *and cherry trees fragrant with blossoms*
> (Song of Solomon 2:11-13 MSG).

Winter can soon be *over* for you as well, my friend. The chilly atmosphere and barren trees around you can be replaced by blossoming flowers and nature's majestic choir of praise.

Whatever you may be going through today, I encourage you to keep on loving, praying, and believing. Sing one more song. Be steadfast and unmovable. Pursue, persist, and press on toward the mark of the high calling of God in Christ Jesus. Lay aside every weight holding you down or holding you back. Don't give up until you receive your breakthrough from God.

The more difficult your winter season has been, the deeper your roots can grow in Christ, and the greater your coming harvest will be. And because of the lessons of the winter season, a whole new beginning can be yours…new joy…new peace…and a new level of contentment in your life in God.

Springtime is just around the corner. A spring of greater vision. A spring of answers to your prayers.

As you await your springtime, continue trusting in God. Continue crying out to Him. Continue believing His promise to work *ALL* things together for your good (Romans 8:28).

Remember: You're not alone in this journey of faith. Everyone needs a breakthrough sometime—and God offers one to YOU *today!*

He wants you all to Himself,
to put His loving, divine arms around you.

CHARLES STANLEY

3

EMBRACE THE LORD OF BREAKTHROUGHS

The closer you get to God, the closer you will be to your breakthrough. How do we know this? Because the Bible describes Him as *"the Lord of Breakthroughs"* or *"the Lord who bursts through"* (1 Chronicles 14:10-11 NLT).

Too often, people seek a breakthrough of some kind without first seeking the Lord. They need a turnaround in their finances, their health, their family, or their emotions, but they're seeking the breakthrough by their own strength and ingenuity. This approach nearly always results in frustration—not because God doesn't want you to have a breakthrough, but because He wants you to receive it from HIM.

King David and other Biblical heroes discovered that God was their Source of every blessing and breakthrough. As a shepherd, David understood that sheep cannot survive very long on their own—they need a shepherd, both to lead them to provision and to rescue them from danger. That's why he joyfully proclaimed, *"The LORD is my shepherd, I shall not want"* (Psalm 23:1).

But David also recognized that he had a role to play in seeking the Lord as his Provider and as the Lord of his breakthroughs: *"Those who seek the LORD shall not lack any good thing"* (Psalm 34:10). He saw that whatever breakthrough he needed, his REAL need was a *"seek the Lord"* need!

The good news is that the Lord of Breakthroughs beckons us to draw near to Him. When we do, He promises to also draw near to us: *"Draw near to God and He will draw near to you"* (James 4:8). And when we come boldly to His throne, He says we will *"find grace to help in time of need"* (Hebrews 4:16).

What resources do you need from Heaven today? More love? More power? More peace? More provision? All of this—and much more—is available when you draw near to the Lord of Breakthroughs today.

THE BATTLE FOR YOUR BREAKTHROUGH

It's important to recognize that breakthroughs seldom come without a battle. In fact, the word "breakthrough" was first used as a military term to signify an offensive thrust past the defensive lines of warfare. The word entered the realm of common speech during the technological age, often used to describe a sudden discovery or invention.

God is first revealed in the Bible as the Lord of Breakthroughs in a military context involving King David. Years earlier, he had conquered the Philistine giant Goliath. But now he is preparing for battle again, facing the Philistine army not far from the site of his famous encounter with the giant.

> *It's important to recognize that breakthroughs seldom come without a battle.*

This time, the Philistines waged their attack in the Valley of Rephaim, which means "the Valley of Giants" or "the Valley of Trouble." Recognizing his need for God's guidance and favor, David paused to pray, asking God for His marching orders:

> *David asked God, "Should I go out to fight the Philistines? Will you hand them over to me?" The Lord replied, "Yes, go ahead. I will hand them over to you."*

> *So David and his troops went up to Baal-perazim and defeated the Philistines there. "God did it!" David exclaimed. "He used me to burst through my enemies like a raging flood!" So they named that place Baal-perazim (which means "the Lord who bursts through")* (1 Chronicles 14:10-11 NLT).

The Philistines abandoned their gods and fled, but they returned again to raid the valley one more time. Even with the memory of the first victory still fresh in his mind, David prayed to the Lord again and listened for His strategy:

> *Once again David asked God what to do. "Do not attack them straight on," God replied. "Instead, circle around behind and attack them near the poplar trees. When you hear a sound like marching feet in the tops of the poplar trees, go out and attack! That will be the signal that God is moving ahead of you to strike down the Philistine army."*
>
> *So David did what God commanded, and they struck down the Philistine army all the way from Gibeon to Gezer. So David's fame spread everywhere, and the Lord caused all the nations to fear David* (1 Chronicles 14:14-17 NLT).

Noticed that David did several crucial things here: He actively sought God's instructions…he listened for what the Lord would say to him…and then *"David DID what God commanded."*

It's a good thing David was listening, for God's strategy this time required a very different response. The Lord rarely does things the same way twice, so it's crucial to receive His instructions before we engage the enemy.

WAIT FOR HIS STRATEGIES

If you need a breakthrough today, make sure to ask God for His battle strategies. His instructions may surprise you, so don't just assume you know what to do.

Seek Him *every* time you need a breakthrough, then obey immediately. You can be certain your Heavenly Father wants to bless you and give you His best. As you wait upon Him, He will not only give you *new strategies,* but He will ALSO give you *new strength* to carry out those strategies (Isaiah 40:31).

God longs for you to experience the great joy of victory, but you must not be discouraged if you encounter a difficult battle before your breakthrough. As you seek the Lord of Breakthroughs and obey His instructions, your "Valley of Trouble" can become the very place where you have a fresh encounter with the One *"who always leads us in triumph"* (2 Corinthians 2:14).

> *God longs for you to experience the great joy of victory, but you must not be discouraged if you encounter a difficult battle before your breakthrough.*

Don't despair if your victory doesn't come right away. In whatever trials you may face, remember Jesus, *"who endured such opposition from sinners, so that you will not grow weary and lose heart"* (Hebrews 12:3 NIV).

It's also crucial not to give up if you encounter failures along the way. Down through history, technological breakthroughs usually occurred only after repeated failures. Thomas Edison reportedly tried unsuccessfully over 10,000 times to invent the electric light bulb before his breakthrough came. The Wright brothers experienced hundreds of crashes before their breakthrough in flight. And numerous scientists performed endless experiments before breakthroughs in DNA research.

If you're struggling to shake off the memories of past failures, remember what God's Word says: *"Though the righteous fall seven times, they rise again"* (Proverbs 24:16 NIV). No matter how far, or how often, you may have fallen, the Lord of Breakthroughs will lift you up and give you victory!

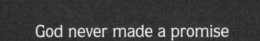

God never made a promise
that was too good to be true.

DWIGHT L. MOODY

4

BE EMPOWERED FOR YOUR BREAKTHROUGH

The ultimate breakthrough comes when you repent of your old ways and ask God to give you a new life in Christ. There might be many other kinds of turnarounds that you need today—perhaps in your health, finances, relationships, or peace of mind. However, it's crucial that you first ask for God's forgiveness and make sure you are living in an obedient relationship with Him.

When Peter preached to the crowd gathered on the day of Pentecost, he concluded his message with an appeal for people to turn from their sins and make sure they had a firm foundation for their new life:

> *"**Repent**, and each of you **be baptized** in the name of Jesus Christ for the forgiveness of your sins; and you will **receive the gift of the Holy Spirit**"* (Acts 2:38).

Peter mentioned repentance as the first step necessary for a new beginning, but he also challenged the crowd to *demonstrate* their repentance by water baptism and then be empowered by the Holy Spirit.

On the Day of Pentecost, God *broke through* by the power of His Spirit, and it's just as important today for every believer to receive this *"power from on high"* (Luke 24:39). Be clear on this: You won't receive a breakthrough or turnaround just by "trying harder" or "turning over a new leaf." God wants you to be filled with His Spirit so you can *"walk in newness of life"* (Romans 6:4).

God wants to empower you to live in victory and abundance. He wants to give you the power of His Spirit, not as a luxury but as a necessity. If you need a breakthrough from God today, don't miss this:

Receiving the power of the Holy Spirit is *essential* to walking victoriously day by day.

You don't have to settle for a powerless and defeated Christian life! Jesus said, *"You **WILL** receive power when the Holy Spirit has come upon you"* (Acts 1:8). Rather than being some kind of strange or spooky spiritual experience, this is a **normal** and **necessary** part of the Christian life.

Paul told the Ephesians, *"Do not get drunk with wine, for that is dissipation, but be filled with the Spirit"* (Ephesians 5:18). If you are struggling with addiction to alcohol, drugs, food, gambling, pornography, or any other kind of bondage today, this is your key to being an overcomer: *"Be filled with the Spirit"*! Instead of being controlled by some kind of addiction, let your life be controlled by the Holy Spirit of God.

POWER TO BREAK FREE

Not only is the Holy Spirit given to us so we'll have power to live the Christian life, but He also delivers us from any demonic bondage or snares of the enemy. Shortly after Jesus was empowered by the Spirit at His baptism by John in the Jordan River, He entered a synagogue and read this Scripture passage from Isaiah:

> *The Spirit of the LORD is upon Me,*
> *Because He anointed Me to preach the gospel to the poor.*
> *He has sent Me to proclaim **release to the captives,***
> *And recovery of sight to the blind,*
> *To **set free those who are oppressed,***
> *To proclaim the favorable year of the LORD* (Luke 4:18).

If you've been a captive to sin or Satan in some area of your life, you need to claim this verse for your situation. By the power of the Holy Spirit, Jesus offers release to captives! And through the anointing of the Spirit, Jesus will *"set free those who are oppressed."* This freedom offered by Jesus is not temporary or transitory, for the Bible declares,

"If the Son sets you free, you will be free indeed" (John 8:36)!

The Good News of the Gospel is that you not only have been forgiven of your sins, but you also have been given power to break free from the dominion of your sins. As a result, you no longer need to live your life in bondage to sin or Satan.

If you are still struggling to break free from the devil's influence in some area of your life, remember these great promises from God's Word:

> *The Son of God appeared for this purpose, to destroy the works of the devil* (1 John 3:8).

> *Greater is He [Jesus] who is in you than he who is in the world [Satan]* (1 John 4:4).

> *I have been crucified with Christ; and it is no longer I who live, but Christ lives in me* (Galatians 2:20).

> *I can do all things through Him who strengthens me* (Philippians 4:13).

Through the power of the Holy Spirit, God offers you the power to be an overcomer! But if you've never asked Him to fill you with His power, you can do so now just by praying this simple prayer:

> *God, thank You for sending Jesus to save me from my sins. Jesus, I want You to be Lord over every area of my life. Thank You for sending Your Holy Spirit so I can be empowered to walk victoriously in a New Beginning with You day by day.*

> *Holy Spirit, in Jesus' name, I invite You to come and fill me up right now. Thank You for Your spiritual gifts and the fruits of love, joy, peace, patience, kindness, goodness, faithfulness, gentleness, and self-control.*

> *Father God, thank You for Your Holy Spirit. Jesus, I pray this prayer in Your powerful name. Amen.*

Faith is taking the first step
even when you don't see the whole staircase.

MARTIN LUTHER KING, JR.

5 LEAVE YOUR PAST BEHIND

You probably have met people who love to live in the past. Day after day, they nurse old wounds and relive past tragedies. They recall in great detail every time they were maligned and mistreated.

Often these people struggle to find intimacy, for they're haunted by memories of trusted people who abused them. It's hard for them to trust God, because they recall a prayer 20 years ago that He didn't seem to answer. And they find it hard to participate in a church, because they can't get over the hypocrisies of other Christians.

What do you say to people who are so bound by the heartaches of their yesterdays that they miss the great plans God has for their life today? How can they shake off the shackles of the past and experience a turn-around from God?

The life of the Prodigal Son reached a turning point when he *"came to himself"* while feeding pigs (Luke 15:17). He realized he was reaping the bitter fruit of his poor choices. If he stayed on his current path, his life would surely continue its downhill slide.

Until a person comes to this kind of moment of realization, he will continue to wallow in the pigpen of yesterday's faults, failures, and hurts. The turning point can't come until we're truly desperate enough to TURN and go in a new direction.

You may be saying, "David, I really *want* a new beginning, but I'm troubled with past sins and failures, and with the hurts and heartaches I've suffered." If the devil is taunting you with such things, I have great news for you: God can get you out of the enemy's pigpen of failure and despair!

Look at these encouraging promises from the book of Isaiah:

> *Behold, the former things have come to pass,*
> *Now I declare new things;*
> *Before they spring forth I proclaim them to you.*
> *Sing to the LORD a new song,*
> *Sing His praise from the end of the earth!*
> (Isaiah 42:9-10)

> *Do not call to mind the former things,*
> *Or ponder things of the past.*
> *Behold, I will do something new,*
> *Now it will spring forth;*
> *Will you not be aware of it?*
> *I will even make a roadway in the wilderness,*
> *Rivers in the desert* (Isaiah 43:18-19).

Some powerful principles are contained in these brief passages of Scripture:

1. God declares His desire to give us a fresh start when we need a breakthrough.

2. He desires to give us a *"new song,"* so we can *"sing His praises from the end of the earth."*

3. He wants to stir our hearts to be *"aware"* of the new things He's doing in our lives.

4. We are told not to *"call to mind"* or *"ponder things of the past."*

5. No matter what kinds of difficult seasons we've been facing, God wants to *"make a roadway in the wilderness, rivers in the desert."*

I encourage you to spend some time meditating on these wonderful promises from God. Instead of the devil's *pigpen*, He wants to show you His *purpose* and *provision*.

PRESSING TOWARD YOUR BREAKTHROUGH

The apostle Paul challenges us to turn our back on the past and then press onward toward our high calling in Christ: *"One thing I do: Forgetting what is behind and straining toward what is ahead"* (Philippians 3:13).

There are several important reasons why you need to forget the past:

- God has told you to leave it behind.

- You cannot change any part of it.

- If you've asked God to forgive you and give you a new beginning, your past sins are forgotten.

- God tells you to forgive anyone who has sinned against you, because you can't be fully released from your past until you release others.

> *Your past is finished, and there's nothing you can do to resurrect it. So bury it and let it stay dead!*

Why worry or fret over something you cannot possibly control? Your past is finished, and there's nothing you can do to resurrect it. So bury it and let it stay dead!

When you repent of your sins, forgive others, and ask God for a breakthrough or new beginning, He forgives and forgets your past misdeeds. Look at what the prophet Micah says about how God handles your sins and your past:

> *Who is a God like You, who pardons iniquity*
> *And passes over the rebellious act of the remnant of*
> *His possession?*
> *He does not retain His anger forever,*
> *Because He delights in unchanging love.*
> *He will again have compassion on us;*

> *He will tread our iniquities under foot.*
> *Yes, You will cast all their sins*
> *Into the depths of the sea* (Micah 7:18-19).

When the Lord forgives you, the Bible says He buries your sins in the deepest part of the ocean! As someone has suggested, God then hangs a "No Fishing" sign to keep us from resurrecting those things ever again.

And notice the word *"all"*: *"You will cast **ALL** their sins into the depths of sea."* Not one of your sins is so terrible that it's unforgiveable. ALL of your sins were included when you asked Jesus Christ to come into your life…when you asked Him to forgive your sins and make you a child of God.

DAVID'S BREAKTHROUGH OF RESTORATION

Like Micah, King David declares that God *"pardons ALL your iniquities"* (Psalm 103:3). At one point in his life, David was under a cloud of shame after committing adultery and murder. Desperately needing a breakthrough of God's grace and mercy, He cried out for forgiveness and restoration:

> *Create in me a clean heart, O God,*
> *And renew a steadfast spirit within me.*
> *Do not cast me away from Your presence*
> *And do not take Your Holy Spirit from me.*
> *Restore to me the joy of Your salvation*
> *And sustain me with a willing spirit* (Psalm 51:10-12).

God heard David's prayer—and He will hear *yours* as well. No matter what kind of pit you have dug for yourself, the Lord can forgive you and give you a fresh start.

How fantastic it is to go from a life of sin and death to a life of joy and peace! David testified of God's amazing grace:

How blessed is he whose transgression is forgiven,
Whose sin is covered!
How blessed is the man to whom the LORD does not
impute iniquity,
And in whose spirit there is no deceit! ...

I acknowledged my sin to You,
And my iniquity I did not hide;
I said, "I will confess my transgressions to the LORD";
And You forgave the guilt of my sin (Psalm 32:1-5).

As far as the east is from the west,
So far has He removed our transgressions from us
(Psalm 103:12).

Your past sins—ALL of them—have been covered by the blood of Jesus. Now it's time for YOU to forget them and leave them in the past, so your turnaround can begin!

As we regularly spend time reading
God's Word and talking to Him in prayer,
we put ourselves in position for Him
to do things in our lives we could
never do on our own.

JOYCE MEYER

6 RECOGNIZE THE POWER OF PRAYING GOD'S WORD

In facing the challenging circumstances of everyday living, the Bible is your lifeline and a vital tool for energizing your prayer life. In order for your prayers to get results, they need to be grounded in faith and filled with the confident expectation that the Lord will be faithful to honor His promises in Scripture.

God makes a fantastic promise about the power and effectiveness of praying His Word: *"So shall My Word be that goes forth from My mouth; it shall **not** return to Me void, but it **shall** accomplish what I please, and it **shall** prosper in the thing for which I sent it"* (Isaiah 55:11).

This is so encouraging. God assures us that when we pray according to His Word and His promises, He will bring it to pass. When we pray God's Word, we're calling on the Lord to honor His promises and breathe *new life* into our circumstances.

And just as it's vital to align our *prayers* with the Word of God, there's also a powerful impact whenever we align our words with the truth of Scripture. That Bible clearly tells us, *"Death and life are in the power of the tongue"* (Proverbs 18:21).

HIS PROMISES ARE FOR YOU!

If you've spent any time at all in reading God's Word, you've surely discovered that it is full of promises. But perhaps you have a lingering doubt when you read the promises in Scripture. "How do I know these promises are really meant for *me?*" you may wonder.

The apostle Paul seems to anticipate this question when he writes:

*"**Whatever** things were written before were written for **our** learning, that **we** through the patience and comfort of the Scriptures might have hope"* (Romans 15:4). Put simply, the truths of Scripture were written with **us** in mind!

Paul says this again in 2 Corinthians 1:18-20:

> *As God is faithful, our word to you was not Yes and No. For the Son of God, Jesus Christ, who was preached among you by us—by me, Silvanus, and Timothy—was not Yes and No, but in Him was Yes. For all the promises of God in Him are Yes, and in Him Amen, to the glory of God through us.*

Do you see how powerful this truth is? In Christ, **ALL** of God's promises are "YES" to *you!*

A FOUNDATION FOR YOUR BREAKTHROUGHS

So, as you get ready to embark on this journey to change your world through prayer, it's important for you to have a Bible that you can underline and write in. In addition to paying special attention to God's promises, you'll also want to note His *conditions* and *instructions* for the fulfillment of those promises.

> *Whenever you need a breakthrough, make a point of looking for promises in the Bible that apply to that specific situation or need.*

Whenever you need a breakthrough, make a point of looking for promises in the Bible that apply to that specific situation or need. You will be amazed by how practical God's Word is to your life today.

We encourage you to buy a journal or notebook where you

can write down what you are learning. Record your prayer requests, and write down your testimonies of God's answers. Years from now, you'll be able to look back and see His faithfulness to hear and answer your prayers!

Are you ready to change your world through prayer? Then let the journey begin. Get ready for some exciting breakthroughs as you claim God's promises and then give Him praise for His answers!

Of all things,
guard against neglecting God in
the secret place of prayer.

WILLIAM WILBERFORCE

7

LEARN THE DISCIPLINE OF PRAYER

Although prayer should come naturally to a person who has been born again by God's Spirit, it also requires WORK. It's an important "spiritual discipline" that requires consistency and persistence.

Despite the wonderful promises the Bible gives us about prayer, many believers are simply unwilling to engage in the hard work required for a successful prayer life. Look at these quotes from some men of God who challenged Christians to be more devoted to prayer:

> *"Spiritual work is taxing work, and men are loath to do it. Praying, true praying, costs an outlay of serious attention and of time, which flesh and blood do not relish."* – E.M. Bounds

> *"The great people of the earth today are the people who pray. I do not mean those who talk about prayer; nor those who say they believe in prayer; nor yet those who can explain about prayer; but I mean those people who take time to pray."* – S.D. Gordon

Are you willing to sacrifice a portion of your time to meet with God each day? This is a vital key to a powerful Christian life! It unlocks the treasure chest of God's wisdom…His guidance…His presence…His power…and His blessings!

Many Christians are satisfied with only praying in church on Sundays and saying "grace" at the dinner table. If this pretty much describes your prayer life, God wants to take you deeper!

GET READY FOR A BATTLE

Of course, the devil will fight you on this each step of the way. He knows the awesome power you have in Jesus' name! If the enemy can discourage you from praying, he has neutralized much of your effectiveness as a warrior for God's Kingdom. You become like a soldier who has been stripped of his weapons and rendered powerless.

Don't let the devil or the busyness of life distract you from a powerful, daily time of prayer! Find a set time of day or night when you can be alone with God without the concerns of the day whirling around in your mind. For some, this may be the first thing in the morning. For others, it may be the last thing before going to bed. The key is to make a daily appointment to meet with God!

If you really want an intimate relationship with God, there are no shortcuts. The way to get to know Him and experience His power is to spend time in His presence.

You may think you don't have the time or energy to pray, but I have found the opposite to be true. It's when I miss my special time of prayer that I feel overwhelmed, fatigued, and under greater attacks from the devil! But after my prayer time, I sense clearer direction from God, renewed energy, and a sense of greater protection from the enemy.

GOING DEEPER

God wants to take your prayer life deeper than the "Now I lay me down to sleep" bedtime rhyme. He wants you to experience the kind of prayer that defeats the devil, heals the sick, raises the dead, restores broken marriages, destroys addictions, delivers the downtrodden, sets the captives free, and glorifies Him!

This kind of prayer life is not wimpy, half-hearted, wishy-washy, or apologetic. It's as bold as a lion, bright as the sun, strong as an ox, and as stable as a mountain. It refuses to give up or back down in the face of adversity.

The Lord wants to bring you into a prayer life that's a delight rather than a drudgery. Instead of the mindless recitation of religious mumbo jumbo, He wants you to experience intimate, heart-to-heart fellowship with Him—the One who is the Lover of your soul and the Ruler of the universe.

TAKING T-I-M-E

Just as it takes time to build a human relationship, Heaven-moving, earth-shaking, hell-defeating prayer requires a commitment of your time. Too many people treat prayer as if God is operating a McPrayer drive-through service where they can place an order, pick it up 10 seconds later, and keep on driving down the road. It doesn't work that way.

Do you really want an intimate relationship with God? There are no shortcuts! The way to get to know Him and experience His power is to spend time in His presence. This comes through praise and worship, reading His Word, and talking with Him in prayer.

Think about it… You can't get to know someone by merely *hearing about* him or her. Getting to know someone requires talking in depth with them. You must spend TIME with them.

Kids today spell love T-I-M-E. "If you really love me," they say, "you'll spend time with me." It's exactly the same in our relationship with God. If you want to demonstrate your love for Him…if you truly want to get to know Him…the most important thing you can do is spend time with Him.

Faith is a living, daring confidence in
God's grace, so sure and certain
that a man could stake his life on it
a thousand times.

MARTIN LUTHER

8

MEDITATE ON THESE THINGS

Sometimes when we pray, we may be expecting God to miraculously touch us and give us some kind of instant revelation. But the Lord rarely taps us on the shoulder with an immediate impartation of knowledge, wisdom, or understanding. Learning one of His lessons usually takes time, study, and prayer.

Please don't be offended by this, but too many Christians are like little birds in a nest, waiting impatiently for their mother to bring them food. Their little mouths are open, and they're chirping, "Hurry, hurry, we're hungry!"

Of course, little birds are helpless and can't do anything to help themselves, but are we? As believers, we can't just passively wait to be fed Scriptural truths by teachers and preachers. We must learn to feed ourselves from God's Word.

While we believe so strongly in the power of prayer, it's just as important to set aside focused times for studying God's Word. If you truly desire to grow in your relationship with the Lord and become more like Him, you *must* do this.

Pastor Charles Stanley has pointed out that "We are either in the process of resisting God's truth or in the process of being shaped and molded by his truth." He specifically ties this "molding" process to learning how to meditate on the Word of God:

> An unschooled man who knows how to meditate
> upon the Lord has learned far more than the man
> with the highest education who does not know how

to meditate. The amount of time we spend with Jesus—meditating on His Word and His majesty, seeking His face—establishes our fruitfulness in the kingdom.

How do we get started on this vital pathway to drawing near to the Lord? Charles Stanley continues: "The essence of meditation is a period of time set aside to contemplate the Lord, listen to Him, and allow Him to permeate our spirits."

Have you set aside a daily time for this? If not, today is a great day to get started!

APPLYING GOD'S TRUTHS TO YOUR LIFE

Many of us have access to a smorgasbord of Christian conventions, Bible studies, church services, and TV preachers. These opportunities can be a real blessing, and many lives are changed because of them. If we wanted to, we could just go from one banqueting table to another, because God's Word is available in so many places in our country.

> *When Scripture doesn't become an integral part of our life, the enemy comes and immediately steals God's promises from us.*

But if we aren't careful, we can become too dependent on this spoon-feeding. It's possible to become so spiritually "fat" that we're useless for anything productive in God's Kingdom.

Just hearing a message and agreeing with it doesn't mean we actually *learned* it. We can admire what was said and even accept God's truth, but until we act upon it, we haven't allowed His truth to become a reality in our lives. We need to stop, meditate on what we've heard, and begin applying it to our lives before moving on to the next lesson God has in store for us.

Many Christians don't practice Scripture meditation, and so they lose much of the benefit they could be gaining from what they read in the Bible or hear preached. The Parable of the Sower in Matthew 13:19 describes this condition: *"When anyone hears the message about the kingdom and does not understand it, the evil one comes and snatches away what was sown in his heart."*

This story is Jesus' explanation of God's Word being sown into our hearts. He describes different types of soil to represent our various human reactions to God's truth. According to this verse, when Scripture doesn't become an integral part of our life, the enemy comes and immediately steals God's promises from us. His goal is to rob us of the most important source of our spiritual growth: God's Word.

THE SPECIAL ROLE OF MEDITATION

Keep in mind that transcendental meditation (a form of Eastern religion) is very different from Biblical meditation. While transcendental meditation is a humanistic mental process involving chanting and incantation, Biblical meditation focuses solely on the Lord and His Word.

This really shouldn't be so controversial, since Scripture clearly tells us to meditate:

> *This Book of the Law shall not depart from your mouth, but you shall **meditate** in it day and night, that you may observe to **do** according to all that is written in it. For then you will make your way prosperous, and then you will have good success* (Joshua 1:8).

> ***Meditate** on these things; give yourself entirely to them, that your progress may be evident to all* (1 Timothy 4:15).

Meditate within your heart on your bed, and be still (Psalm 4:4).

*Finally, brethren, whatever things are true, whatever things are noble, whatever things are just, whatever things are pure, whatever things are lovely, whatever things are of good report, if there is any virtue and if there is anything praiseworthy—**meditate** on these things* (Philippians 4:8).

In all of these verses, we are instructed and encouraged to use our minds to apply the truths of God's Word to our lives. We are told to meditate on the Lord, His Word, and the things of His Kingdom.

A COMMON BIBLICAL PRACTICE

Meditation is a spiritual discipline very familiar to the Biblical writers:

*His delight is in the law of the LORD, and in His law he **meditates** day and night* (Psalm 1:2).

*When I remember You on my bed, I **meditate** on You in the night watches* (Psalm 63:6).

*I will also **meditate** on all Your work, and talk of Your deeds* (Psalm 77:12).

*I will **meditate** on Your precepts, and contemplate Your ways* (Psalm 119:15).

*Your servant **meditates** on Your statutes* (Psalm 119:23).

*My eyes are awake through the night watches, that I may **meditate** on Your word* (Psalm 119:148).

*I **meditate** on all Your works; I muse on the work of Your hands* (Psalm 143:5).

> *I will **meditate** on the glorious splendor of Your majesty, and on Your wondrous works* (Psalm 145:5).

> *A book of remembrance was written before Him for those who fear the LORD and who **meditate** on His name* (Malachi 3:16).

With so many references in the Bible to meditation, isn't it amazing we don't hear more about it in the church today? Yet this is an important tool as we pursue greater intimacy with the Lord and greater application of His Word in our lives.

SETTING ASIDE SPECIAL TIME

When we devote extended time to meditation, it can be wonderful!

Although it may not be easy to find time for meditation, this is worth the fight for you to keep growing in your relationship with the Lord.

Some meditation time can be focused on prayer, but some of it can be spent just reflecting on the many questions you want to ask God. Taking the time to think these through and look up what the Bible has to say about them can cause meditation to feel like a luxury, and it will create an even greater hunger for you to spend time doing this in the future.

Although it may not be easy to find time for meditation, this is worth the fight for you to keep growing in your relationship with the Lord.

Barbara and I so enjoy meditating on God's Word and searching for His answers to the questions on our hearts. It's a wonderful chance for us to be our true selves and experience peace and safety in His presence. We always come away relaxed and refreshed from this special time of communion with Him.

FINDING A SPECIAL PLACE

Just as we need to set aside special times for prayer and meditation, it also helps to have a special place where we can get away for undistracted fellowship with the Lord. This is beautifully portrayed in a short story by David Wolfe entitled, "Teaching Your Children About God":

> *There was a rabbi who had a son. It was soon noticed by the man that the young boy was often in the forest near their house. The boy's father had become worried since he wasn't sure of the dangers his son might face.*
>
> *He decided to speak to the boy about this, and asked him why he was spending so much time alone in the forest. The boy replied that he was going there to find God.*
>
> *The rabbi, happy to hear that his son was in search of the Divine, noted that the boy didn't have to go into the woods to find God, "Because," he added, "God is the same everywhere."*
>
> *The boy's answer?*
>
> *"Yes, Dad, but I am not."*

It's easy to identify with the boy. Some people may not understand why you love to get away with your Bible and be alone as you meditate on God's Word...but that's okay. Alone time with Him provides a fantastic opportunity for you to truly be "you."

God can be so real to you when you're alone with Him. You can cry or laugh, and you don't have to explain yourself to anyone! You can clear away all the cobwebs from your heart and mind, and then truly experience and hear from the Lord as you meditate on His Word.

We receive many requests from our Inspiration Partners who want us to pray they will grow closer to the Lord...and we do. However, we always want them to understand that they must be dedicated and disciplined in setting aside their own time to study and meditate on God's Word.

Know this: Absolutely none of the time you spend with the Lord and His Word will be wasted. You always will come away renewed and refreshed!

The little estimate
we put on prayer is evident
from the little time we give to it.

E.M. BOUNDS

9 EXPECT RESULTS FROM YOUR PRAYERS

Too often, people see prayer as merely a superstition, something akin to a rabbit's foot or four-leaf clover. Although they pray, they don't really expect anything to happen.

However, this is NOT at all how the Bible describes the prayers of God's people. We must pray in FAITH and *expect results* from our prayers. Why? Because God is faithful, and He has given us incredible promises about the power we have in prayer.

Believers throughout history have discovered that prayer could change their personal life, their loved ones, and the world around them. E.M. Bounds once wrote, "God shapes the world by prayer. The more praying there is in the world the better the world will be, the mightier the forces against evil."

So what about *you?* When you pray, do you truly expect things to change?

Nineteenth–century revivalist Charles Finney pointed out that God wants our prayers to be *effective*—not just empty religious exercises: "Effective prayer is prayer that attains what it seeks. It is prayer that moves God, affecting its end."

Think of it: ***Your prayers literally can move God to action!*** As Alfred Lord Tennyson wrote, "More things are wrought by prayer than this world dreams of."

PRODUCING "WONDERFUL RESULTS"

So why don't we pray more often, expecting greater results? F.B. Meyer correctly observed, "The greatest tragedy of life is not unanswered prayer, but unoffered prayer."

One of the great Scriptural promises about prayer is found in James 5:16 (NLT): *"The earnest prayer of a righteous person has **great power** and **produces wonderful results.**"* Other translations say that the fervent prayer of a righteous man *"avails much."*

Put simply, God wants us to learn how to pray prayers that bring the desired results—blessing our lives, touching our loved ones, and changing our world.

However, we meet many people who doubt whether God is listening to their prayers. Maybe you're feeling like this today, wondering whether the Lord really cares about your situation. Perhaps you're tired of waiting for your breakthrough, and you've concluded that your prayers aren't making a difference.

You may be surprised that many people in Biblical times had the same thoughts. The prophet Jeremiah was so distressed by his circumstances that he once said to God: *"Your help seems as uncertain as a seasonal brook, like a spring that has gone dry"* (Jeremiah 15:18 NLT). And faced with a fierce storm, Jesus' disciples complained, *"Teacher, do You not care that we are perishing?"* (Mark 4:38) They accused Jesus of not caring about their situation!

However, the good news is that the Lord DOES care about our circumstances. He wants to quiet our storms…break through in our finances…heal our bodies…and restore our broken relationships.

The Bible describes Jesus as our great high priest, who *"always lives to make intercession"* for us (Hebrews 7:25). And we're told that *"we have not an high priest which cannot be touched with the feeling of our infirmities"* (Hebrews 4:15 KJV). So we never need to wonder whether Jesus truly cares about our difficult circumstances. He does!

DECLARING THE MIRACLE BEFORE IT COMES

What does it look like to *expect results* from our prayers? We love the story in Mark 5:25-34 about a woman who had struggled with a hemorrhage for 12 long years. Because of her type of illness, she was considered "unclean" and an outcast. And despite spending all her money on doctors, this woman's condition had only gotten worse. She was desperate for a miracle.

Perhaps you are feeling much the same way today. You've looked everywhere…tried everything…spent all you have…and still your condition remains.

But the woman in this story was confident that, with just one touch, she would be instantly healed by Jesus. If fact, she declared her healing the moment she heard that Jesus was coming her way: *"If only I may touch His clothes, I shall be made well"* (v. 28).

You see, the woman faced a crucial choice. She had been disappointed by the doctors for many years, so it must have been difficult to believe that this stranger named Jesus could relieve her condition. However, faith rose in her heart, and she put that faith in action. Pressing through the crowd, she touched the hem of Jesus' garment, and the result was amazing: *"Immediately the fountain of her blood was dried up, and she felt in her body that she was healed of the affliction"* (v. 29).

> *Your prayers must reflect an active, confident faith that expects miracles when you reach out to touch the Lord.*

Friend, you have a similar choice to make. You can get discouraged and just give up, or you can press through your circumstances and reach out to Jesus for your miracle.

Yes, you can change your world through prayer. But this doesn't mean wishy-washy, passive prayers. Your prayers must reflect the kind of faith this woman displayed—an active, confident faith that expects miracles when you reach out to touch the Lord.

Prayer is simply a
two-way conversation between
you and God.

BILLY GRAHAM

10 CHANGE YOUR PERSPECTIVE ON PRAYER

Do you need a miracle from God today? Perhaps you are seeking a physical healing, a better job, a financial blessing, or a restored relationship with a loved one. If so, you may be tempted to think it would require *great effort* for the Lord to give you a "big" breakthrough like that.

But the Bible offers great news for you! God is a miracle-working God, so it's not difficult at all for Him to perform miracles. Remember: In order to create the universe, He merely had to *speak a word,* and that's all He needs to do to change your circumstances today.

In Matthew 15:21-28, a Canaanite woman came to Jesus with a need: *"Have mercy on me, O Lord, Son of David! My daughter is severely demon-possessed"* (v. 22). Even though she cried out in desperation, Jesus *"answered her not a word"* (v. 23).

The Lord explained that He was only sent *"to the lost sheep of the house of Israel"* (v. 24). In other words, the focus of His ministry was on the Jews. Because this woman was a Gentile, she simply didn't qualify.

This was a test. Would this woman *persist* in her request, or would she back down and give up?

Friend, you may be undergoing a similar test of your faith today. Perhaps you've prayed about a serious need in your life, but God hasn't seemed to respond. What will you do?

Well, the Canaanite woman wasn't about to take "No" for an answer. She continually cried out, *"Lord, help me!"* (v. 25)

At this point, Jesus made a very interesting statement: *"It is not good to take the children's bread and throw it to the little dogs"* (v. 26). Again, He was saying that "the children" (the Jews) were to receive their food first (compare Romans 1:16).

Many people would have lost all hope at Jesus' stern reply, but not this woman. *"Yes, Lord,"* she said, *"yet even the little dogs eat the crumbs which fall from their masters' table"* (v. 27).

> *Your prayer request is not too much to ask of God — it's just a "crumb" in comparison to the vast resources of Heaven.*

This statement changed everything. Jesus commended her faith and granted her request: *"'O woman, great is your faith! Let it be to you as you desire.' And her daughter was healed from that very hour"* (v. 28).

HOW DOES JESUS *SEE* OUR FAITH?

Why was Jesus so impressed by the Canaanite woman's faith? There are several reasons.

First, this woman was *persistent*, even though it meant being quite bothersome to Jesus and His disciples. And when her request initially was denied, she refused to back off or give up. It may seem surprising that Jesus wasn't upset by her tenacious, somewhat rude, attitude. Instead, He *applauded* it.

The second lesson from this story is that Jesus could *see* the woman's faith by her *words* and her *actions*. Many people claim to have faith for God's miracles in their life, yet their words and actions are a complete contradiction.

Apply this test to your own life: If someone spent a week listening to your words and examining your behavior, would they be impressed that you were trusting God for your miracle breakthrough? If not, the Lord wants to do a work in your heart today.

The third lesson is perhaps the most profound: The Canaanite woman understood that the miracle she sought was merely a "crumb" from the Master's table. In other words, she didn't see her request as anything difficult for Jesus…

A mere CRUMB was all she needed for her breakthrough!

Do you grasp how powerful this truth is? *Whatever* your need may be today, it's no big deal for God to fix. Your prayer request is not "too much to ask" of Him—it's just a crumb in comparison to the vast resources of Heaven.

So go ahead and cry out to Jesus as this woman did. Boldly tell Him your need. One small morsel from His table will transform your situation in an instant!

Any concern too small to be
turned into a prayer
is too small to be made into a burden.

CORRIE TEN BOOM

11 TAKE YOUR PROBLEM TO THE JUDGE

In Luke 18, Jesus told the story of a widow who sought justice for a difficult circumstance in her life. Through this parable, Jesus was describing an important key for how you are to approach your Heavenly Father with your petitions.

Unable to resolve the situation on her own, the woman in this story decided to seek help from a local judge. Unfortunately, however, the judge *"did not fear God nor regard man"* (v. 2). In other words, he was heartless and corrupt, with no intention of helping her.

But this widow persisted until the unjust judge gave her relief. *"Though I do not fear God nor regard man,"* he reasoned, *"yet because this widow troubles me I will avenge her, lest by her continual coming she weary me"* (v. 4-5).

There are three characters in this story:

- The *woman*, who represents us

- The *judge*, who represents God (even though He is loving, kind, and just—nothing like the judge in this story)

- The woman's *adversary*, which represents her need or problem

Perhaps you are facing an *"adversary"* today, much like the woman in Jesus' story. This may be an overwhelming load of debt, a wayward son or daughter, a bout of fear or depression, or a severe health problem. Whatever challenge you face, you may find it tempting to lose heart, to grow weary in well-doing, and to doubt whether your adversary will ever be defeated.

But when you get to that point, you need to take your case to the Judge! He's the key to your victory. So instead of wearing yourself out by battling your opponent in your own strength, recognize that *"the battle is not yours, but God's"* (2 Chronicles 20:15).

JESUS, OUR ADVOCATE

Jesus is your *"advocate with the Father"* (1 John 2:1)! He's your perfect attorney, the one who pleads your case with the Judge in Heaven. What better attorney could you possibly ask for?

Everything changes when you go to the Judge with your need. God has the power to solve your problems and defeat your opponents.

So how did this woman get results from the judge? First, she *troubled* him. Second, she came to the judge *continually*, pushing him to the limit until he agreed to listen and respond. Third, she *wearied* him. Jesus used a word meaning "to beat black and blue (like a boxer buffets his body) or to create an intolerable annoyance."

> *We must hang on to God until His blessing comes and we receive the breakthrough we need.*

This is a vivid description of intense persistence. Jesus said we should approach our Heavenly God with this kind of tenacity—even if it means wearing Him out and becoming an intolerable annoyance. What a stunning model for how we're to approach God in prayer!

Jesus concluded this parable by promising that God will *"avenge His own elect who cry out day and night to Him"* (v. 7). The word used here for cry means "to speak with a loud voice, to cry to one for help, to implore someone's aid." Clearly, we must boldly raise our voice and express our needs to the Lord.

Remember this: No man, no church, no denomination, no ministry can save you, heal you, or answer your prayers. But there is a Judge, and He's your Heavenly Father. He gladly hears and answers prayer, and His Son Jesus is your Advocate, constantly praying for you. Pause for a moment and give Him thanks for being your Advocate and faithful intercessor (Hebrews 7:25)!

GETTING VIOLENT IN YOUR PRAYERS

God's Word never advocates coming to God with timid, polite, quiet little prayer. To the contrary, Jesus said, *"From the days of John the Baptist until now the kingdom of heaven suffers violence, and the violent take it by force"* (Matthew 11:12).

The word here translated "violence" means "to force or be seized." The word translated "violent" means "the forcer or the energetic." And "take it" means "to seize, pluck, pull, or take it" by force.

Jesus is telling us that He wants us to be forceful rather than passive. As we seek to advance His purposes, we must be energetic to seek, seize, and take His Kingdom by force.

This includes not just crying out to Him, but also putting our faith into action. It means getting spiritually violent. Like Jacob, we must be willing to wrestle with God all night and then say, *"I will not let You go unless You bless me"* (Genesis 32:26).

Perhaps you've heard this described as the **P.U.S.H.** principle: We must **P**ray **U**ntil **S**omething **H**appens! We must hang on to God until His blessing comes and we receive the breakthrough we need.

DANIEL'S PERSISTENCE

The prophet Daniel once prayed for 20 days with no answer. Still he believed God and persisted in his prayers. Perhaps Daniel felt discouraged at times or bewildered about why God seemingly hadn't responded to his prayers, yet he didn't give up!

Finally, Daniel's answer came on the 21st day. His persistence and time seeking God were rewarded—and the same will happen as you persistently pray for YOUR breakthrough.

Today, by faith, let's join together in crying out to God, our righteous Judge. Let's put our faith into action and believe He will answer our prayers. Instead of quitting or becoming discouraged, let's keep praying and seeking God.

And let's never forget Jesus' central lesson in this story: *"Men always ought to pray and not lose heart"* (Luke 18:1). We must not let discouragement stop us when we're on the brink of a breakthrough!

Prayer is as natural an
expression of faith
as breathing is of life.

JONATHAN EDWARDS

12

UTILIZE THE DIVERSE TYPES OF PRAYER

When God gave Moses instructions for building the Tabernacle in the wilderness, He told him the exact specifications, what furniture to include, what was to be inside. The Bible says Moses fashioned the furniture in the Tabernacle after the pattern he saw in Heaven (Exodus 25:9).

One of the pieces of furniture Moses saw in Heaven was the Altar of Incense. This altar symbolized the prayers of God's people ascending before Him to Heaven.

David said in Psalm 141:1-2, *"Give ear to my voice when I cry out to You. Let my prayer be set before You as incense."* And God said in Exodus 30:8, *"When Aaron lights the lamps at twilight, he shall burn incense on it, a **perpetual incense** before the LORD throughout your generations."*

Think of it: Our incense of prayer and worship is supposed to ascend to the Lord *perpetually*. Instead of just being a random activity, prayer is meant to be our *way of life* as we practice God's presence continuously. As Paul wrote in 1 Thessalonians 5:17, we are called to *"pray without ceasing."*

God instructed the Israelites to use 11 different types of spices on the Altar of Incense. Interestingly enough, we've found 11 different types of prayer spoken about in the New Testament. Perhaps you can find more, but we've found these 11:

1. Prayer of PETITION

"If we know that He hears us, whatever we ask, we know that we have the petitions that we have asked of Him." – 1 John 5:15

2. Prayer of FAITH

"The prayer of faith will save the sick, and the Lord will raise him up." – James 5:15

3. Prayer IN THE SPIRIT

"Praying always with all prayer and supplication in the Spirit." – Ephesians 6:18

4. Prayer of THANKSGIVING

"Be anxious for nothing, but in everything by prayer and supplication, with thanksgiving, let your requests be made known to God." – Philippians 4:6

5. Prayer of AGREEMENT

"If two of you agree on earth concerning anything that they ask, it will be done for them by My Father in heaven." – Matthew 18:19

6. Prayer of BINDING

"I will give you the keys of the kingdom of heaven, and whatever you bind on earth will be bound in heaven, and whatever you loose on earth will be loosed in heaven." – Matthew 16:19

7. Prayer of LOOSING

Matthew 16:19 *(see above)*

8. Prayer of INTERCESSION

"I have prayed for you, that your faith should not fail; and when you have returned to Me, strengthen your brethren." – Luke 22:32

9. Prayer of UNDERSTANDING

"I will pray with the spirit, and I will also pray with the understanding." – 1 Corinthians 14:15

10. Prayer of JUDGMENT

"When He opened the fifth seal, I saw under the altar the souls of those who had been slain for the word of God and for the testimony which they held. And they cried with a loud voice, saying, 'How long, O Lord, holy and true, until You judge and avenge our blood on those who dwell on the earth?'" – Revelation 6:9-11

11. Prayer of HEALING

"Confess your trespasses to one another, and pray for one another, that you may be healed. The effective, fervent prayer of a righteous man avails much."
– James 5:16

> *If we can just catch a glimpse of our Heavenly Father, every need will be met, every longing will be satisfied.*

Take another look at this list, asking God to show you the specific types of prayer that will unlock the breakthroughs you presently need. Whatever problem you face, God has an answer as you draw near to Him through prayer.

One of Jesus' disciples, Philip, made a powerful request of Him: *"Lord, show us the Father. That is all we need"* (John 14:8 NCV). In other words, if we can just catch a glimpse of our Heavenly Father, every need will be met, every longing will be satisfied.

David said it this way: *"Those who seek the LORD shall not lack any good thing"* (Psalm 34:10). So whatever need we have today, our REAL need is a *"seek the Lord"* need!

"LORD, TEACH US TO PRAY"

In Luke 11:1, Jesus' disciples made an amazing request: *"Lord, teach us to pray."* They could have asked Him for many other things, such as, "Teach us to preach…teach us to heal the sick…teach us to cast out demons...or teach us to feed the multitudes." But, instead, the disciples realized that *prayer* was the secret of Jesus' life and ministry. If only they could learn to pray like Jesus prayed, everything else would fall into place.

Yet no one has a powerful prayer life automatically. Prayer is an art we must *learn*, something we must *grow in* daily.

Barbara and I have devoted ourselves to prayer over the years, and it's the foundation of everything we do at Inspiration Ministries. Along the way, we've learned many important truths about prayer. Here are just a few:

- Prayer is work. It will cost you time, attention, energy, and significant sacrifice.

- In order to grow in your prayer life, you will need discipline, practice, cultivation, and determination.

- In order to get results, your prayers must be fervent, passionate, persistent, and unashamed.

- Sin will undermine your prayer life and block God's answers. He wants us to come to Him with *"clean hands and a pure heart"* (Psalm 24:3-4).

- Prayer is habit-forming and must become second nature to you.

- Unbelief will undercut the effectiveness of your prayers, but when prayer is coupled with true faith, it "sees" the answer coming before it arrives.

- Breakthroughs in prayer sometimes require becoming spiritually violent.

- Effectiveness in prayer requires that you seek alignment with God's will.

- Your faith must be combined with *patience*, and you must recognize that God has an appointed time for everything.

- Unforgiveness is one of the biggest hindrances to answered prayer (Matthew 5:23, Mark 11:25).

- Sometimes your breakthroughs in prayer are delayed until you take a step of faith and obedience, such as sowing a financial seed into God's Kingdom.

Take a few minutes now to consider your own experiences in prayer. What have you learned so far? What areas does God want you to still grow in?

Remember: Whether you are a seasoned prayer warrior or just a novice on your journey to a powerful prayer life, you can make this request of Jesus: "Lord, teach me to pray." He will help you take the next step in changing your world through prayer.

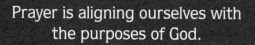

Prayer is aligning ourselves with
the purposes of God.

E. STANLEY JONES

13 MOVE GOD'S HAND THROUGH PRAYER

Let's be clear: It is more important to seek God's face than to seek His hand. He promises that if we *"draw near"* to Him, He will draw near to us (James 4:8). And when we seek His Kingdom first, everything else will be provided for us (Matthew 6:33).

But even though our main focus in prayer should not be on "getting God to do what we want Him to do," the Bible is full of examples of men and women who literally moved the Lord's hand through their fervent prayers. Sometimes this is even referred to as God changing His mind!

- Abraham negotiated with God about sparing Sodom if there were even 10 righteous people there (Genesis 18:22-33).

- After Moses interceded for the wayward Israelites, the Bible says that *"the LORD changed His mind about the harm which He said He would do to His people"* (Exodus 32:14 NASB).

- In Numbers 14:20, God changed His mind again and spared the rebellious Israelites from the judgment and destruction He had planned for them. The key again was Moses' intercession.

- In 2 Kings 20, King Hezekiah was *"sick and near death."* In fact, God told him, *"Set your house in order, for you shall die, and not live"* (v. 1). However, when Hezekiah cried out to the Lord in prayer, God changed His mind and added 15 years to his life.

There are other Scriptural examples as well, but these will help you understand the power of fervent prayer and intercession to literally change God's mind and move His hand. These acts of intercession are described in various ways:

- Pleading with the Lord (Exodus 32:11)

- Reminding God of His promises (Exodus 32:12-14)

- Repenting and returning to the Lord (Leviticus 26:31, Numbers 14:19, Deuteronomy 30:2-3)

- Being contrite and broken (Psalm 51:17, Isaiah 66:2)

- Humbling ourselves before God (Leviticus 26:41)

- Seeking God's face and turning from our wicked ways (2 Chronicles 7:14)

- Coming into God's presence with *"clean hands a pure heart"* (Psalms 24:3-5)

- Returning to the Lord (2 Chronicles 6:38-39)

- Waiting on the Lord (Isaiah 64:4, Isaiah 40:31)

- Fasting (Isaiah 58)

- Bringing God a special offering or sacrifice (1 Chronicles 21)

When we examine the examples of those who received break-throughs in their circumstances through prayer, it soon becomes apparent that God wants something much more than shallow "Now I lay me down to sleep" prayers. He wants us to come BOLDLY to His throne of grace (Hebrews 4:16), asking Him to intervene in our lives in miraculous ways. No request is too small, nor is any need too great.

DEALING WITH BARRIERS TO EFFECTIVE PRAYER

In order to change your world through prayer, you must recognize the barriers that may be blocking God's answers to your prayers. For example, the psalmist wrote, *"If I regard iniquity in my heart, the Lord will not hear"* (Psalm 66:18).

Make no mistake about it: Unconfessed sin in your life will hinder the effectiveness of your prayers. The Bible warns that when we refuse to listen to the Lord, He will refuse to listen to us (Zechariah 7:13).

God told us in Isaiah 1:15-17:

> *When you spread out your hands, I will hide My eyes from you; even though you make many prayers, I will not hear. Your hands are full of blood. Wash yourselves, make yourselves clean; put away the evil of your doings from before My eyes. Cease to do evil, learn to do good; seek justice...*

Isaiah later described both God's desire to hear His people's prayer and also the fact that sin often will block those answers:

> *Behold, the LORD's hand is not shortened, that it cannot save; nor His ear heavy, that it cannot hear. But your iniquities have separated you from your God; and your sins have hidden His face from you, so that He will not hear* (Isaiah 59:1-2).

Unconfessed sin in your life will hinder the effectiveness of your prayers.

Take a few minutes right now to ask the Lord to search your heart and reveal any area of sin or disobedience that may be blocking His blessings in your life.

This is a serious matter! The Bible describes severe consequences when we refuse to acknowledge and repent of sin:

- Enemies rise up against us and defeat us (1 Kings 8:33, Deuteronomy 28:47-52).

- The heavens are shut up, and instead of rain and provision, there is famine and pestilence (1 Kings 8:35-37).

- We're more prone to disease and sickness (1 Kings 8:32, Deuteronomy 28:21-22).

- We'll suffer from emotional turmoil, such as confusion, fear, and depression (Deuteronomy 28:20-29, Genesis 4:6-7).

- The enemy will attack our family (Deuteronomy 28:30-32)

- We'll be taken into captivity (Deuteronomy 28:68)

Fortunately, we can turn to the Lord in prayer and repentance, so we don't have to experience these calamities. As we *"diligently obey the voice of the LORD,"* we can experience His incredible blessings instead of these curses (Deuteronomy 28:1-14).

To love means loving
the unlovable.

To forgive means pardoning
the unpardonable.

GILBERT K. CHESTERTON

14 DON'T FORGET TO FORGIVE

Another major hindrance to answered prayer is a failure to forgive those who have wronged us. If you've ever played the popular board game, *Monopoly*, you've probably received a "Get Out of Jail Free" card. Instead of trying to pay your way out of jail, that single card was your ticket to instant freedom.

Although many believers don't realize it, God has given each of us a "Get Out of Jail Free" card. Jesus' death on the Cross makes it possible for us to escape from our prison of sin and death! People may try all sorts of other things to help them overcome their winter season and find a new beginning, but only Jesus' blood can truly cleanse our sins and set us free.

As Robert Lowry says in the beloved old hymn:

> *What can wash away my sin?*
> *Nothing but the blood of Jesus.*
> *What can make me whole again?*
> *Nothing but the blood of Jesus.*
>
> *O precious is the flow*
> *That makes me white as snow;*
> *No other fount I know;*
> *Nothing but the blood of Jesus.*

If God has forgiven your shortcomings and sins, why should YOU remember them? If the devil keeps sowing condemnation in your life by bringing up your painful or sinful past, remember this: The devil is a liar! God's Word says, *"There is therefore now NO condemnation for those who are in Christ Jesus"* (Romans 8:1)!

On the Cross, Jesus bore all your fears, guilt, and shame…so YOU don't have to bear them any longer! Once you grasp this truth, you will not only be free from the "jailhouse" of your past, but also free to go forward in God and experience a new beginning in Him.

What a blessing to receive God's "Get Out of Jail Free" card! So toss out any guilt, fear, shame, or condemnation, and come into God's presence with praise and worship on your lips!

Psalm 103:10-13 says:

> He has not dealt with us according to our sins, nor rewarded us according to our iniquities. For as high as the heavens are above the earth, so great is His lovingkindness towards those who fear Him. As far as the east is from the west, so far has He removed our transgressions from us. Just as a father has compassion on his children, so the Lord has compassion on those who fear Him.

The message is clear: God loves you and offers you total and complete forgiveness.

> *God has graciously forgiven our sins, and He doesn't want us to allow unforgiveness toward others to bring us back into a spiritual prison.*

DON'T GO BACK TO JAIL!

It breaks God's heart that many of His children have gone back to "jail." He has graciously forgiven their sins, but they've allowed unforgiveness toward others to bring them back into a spiritual prison.

In Matthew 18:21-35, Jesus tells a sobering story about a man who was forgiven from a huge debt, but who refused to forgive someone who owed him a much smaller amount. The man had come before his master to plead for mercy, and the master was gracious to him: *"The master of that servant was moved with compassion, released him, and forgave him the debt"* (v. 27).

Friend, this is exactly what the Lord has done for YOU in Jesus' death on the Cross…

- He showed His compassion for you.
- He forgave your debt of sin.
- He released you from the prison of your past.

Unfortunately, though, this story doesn't have a happy ending. This man who received such mercy refused to forgive someone who owed him a very small debt:

> *That servant went out and found one of his fellow servants who owed him a hundred denarii; and he laid hands on him and took him by the throat, saying, "Pay me what you owe!" So his fellow servant fell down at his feet and begged him, saying, "Have patience with me, and I will pay you all." And he would not, but went and threw him into prison till he should pay the debt* (vs. 28-30).

Notice that forgiving others is a choice, not a feeling. When asked for mercy, he was unwilling to give it. Although he had been set free from his own debt, he chose to put the other man in prison.

However, the master of the first servant was irate when he heard about this:

> *Then his master, after he had called him, said to him, "You wicked servant! I forgave you all that debt because you begged me. Should you not also have had compassion on your fellow servant, just as I had pity on you?"* (vs. 32-33)

The master's anger resulted in terrible consequences for the man who refused to forgive: *"His master was angry, and delivered him to the torturers until he should pay all that was due to him"* (v. 34).

Jesus ends this story with a pointed warning about the consequences of unforgiveness: *"My heavenly Father will also do the same to you, if each of you does not forgive his brother from your heart"* (v. 35).

ARE YOU BEING TORMENTED?

Jesus' story says those who hold on to unforgiveness will be handed over to *"torturers."* Other translations say *"tormenters"* or *"jailers."*

This isn't God's will for our lives! Jesus died to set us free from jail…free from guilt, shame, and torment. But our unwillingness to forgive others will bring us back into a jailhouse of our own making. The "Get Out of Jail Free" card will only work when we have forgiven everyone who has wronged us.

Perhaps you are being tormented by your past…your failures and mistakes…or the ways you've been victimized by another person. If so, God wants to wrap His love around you today—yet He still requires you to forgive those who have wronged you.

Jesus' story is an illustration of a warning He gives in the Sermon on the Mount. After instructing us to pray, *"Forgive us our debts, as we also have forgiven our debtors"* (Matthew 6:12), Jesus adds, *"For if you forgive others for their transgressions, your heavenly Father will also forgive you. But if you do not forgive others, then your Father will not forgive your transgressions"* (vs. 14-15).

Many people today are being tormented by their past…their failures and mistakes…or the ways they've been victimized by another person. Sometimes the past traumas are very real, very severe, and very painful. Perhaps you've been victimized by an abusive relationship or a dishonest business partner. If so, God wants to wrap His love and compassion around you today—yet He still requires you to forgive the person who wronged you.

If you find yourself in a place of torment today, God wants to release you. But the key to your prison is in your *own* hand. We encourage you today to get away for some time with the Lord, asking Him to work His forgiveness in your heart. As long as it takes, spend time choosing to forgive each person who has hurt you. Tear up every "IOU," and release them from their debts.

OFFENSES AND OBJECTIONS

Perhaps you've been holding on to your offenses for a long time. Someone has hurt you deeply, and you feel justified in holding an angry grudge against them. If so, there are two things you must remember:

1. **The main person hurt by your offense is not the other person, it's YOU!**

2. **As severely as you have been wronged, your trauma is no greater than was experienced by many men and women of God in the Bible:**

   • Because of the jealousy of his brothers, **Joseph** was thrown into the bottom of a well, became a slave in Egypt, and spent years in a dungeon. Yet he chose to forgive his brothers and welcome them into the prosperity God had given him. *Instead of taking revenge against his brothers, Joseph told them, "You meant evil against me, but God meant it for good"* (Genesis 50:20).

   • **Job** found a wonderful reversal of his fortunes when he prayed for his friends—even though they had spent many days badgering and criticizing him (Job 42:10-12).

   • **Naomi** and **Ruth** faced grief and uncertainty after their husbands died, yet God gave them a wonderful new beginning when they moved back to Judah (Ruth 1:1-22).

- The **Samaritan woman at the well** (John 4:1-42) and the woman caught in adultery (John 8:1-11) both endured trauma at the hands of men and because of their own foolish choices—but they each received a new beginning when Jesus forgave and restored them.

- **Stephen** forgave those who were stoning him to death: *"Lord, do not hold this sin against them!"* (Acts 7:54-60) This act of forgiveness was one of the primary factors leading to the conversion of the apostle Paul.

- **Jesus**, while carrying the sins of the world on His back on the Cross, issued a powerful word of forgiveness that has echoed down through the centuries: *"Father, forgive them; for they do not know what they are doing"* (Luke 23:34).

So remember this when you're tempted to throw yourself a pity party and hold on to offenses toward others: God wants you to follow Jesus' example and forgive those who have treated you unjustly.

HURTFUL WAYS

Forgiveness often is very difficult, but it's an essential key to your new beginning. Your winter season will go on forever unless you make a decision to forgive everyone who has hurt you.

David prayed, *"Search me, O God, and know my heart; try me and know my anxious thoughts; and see if there be any **hurtful way** in me"* (Psalm 139:23-24). Make no mistake about it, unforgiveness is a *"hurtful way"* that will imprison you with torment unless you deal with it.

A few years ago, Barbara and I spent time with a pastor friend of ours. He mentioned that each month he goes away for a few days to spend time with the Lord.

Barbara and I asked him what he did on these personal retreats, and he told us he always starts by asking the Lord to show him anyone he hadn't forgiven yet. Our friend shared that on one of these retreats, he spent *three whole days* forgiving people who had wronged him!

Like this pastor, don't just *assume* you've forgiven people who have hurt you. You may need to spend some time asking God to search your heart. If you're still *talking about* the offense—months or even years after it occurred—it's likely that you still have some forgiving to do.

Take time today to allow the Lord to search your heart and remove any *"hurtful way"* or unforgiveness that is keeping you imprisoned to your past.

LET GO!

The story has been told about a mom who baked some chocolate chip cookies for her young son. "Tommy," she told him, "I'm putting the cookies in the cookie jar, but you can have some after dinner."

> *Take time today to allow the Lord to search your heart and remove any "hurtful way" or unforgiveness that is keeping you imprisoned to your past.*

Of course, Tommy couldn't wait for this special treat. While his mom was in the other room, Tommy opened the cookie jar and reached in to grab a few big cookies. However, when he tried to remove his hand, he discovered that it was stuck.

Tommy began to cry and then screamed to his mom, "HELP! I'M TRAPPED!"

When Tommy's mom ran into the room, she saw that his hand was stuck, and he was sobbing hysterically. She decided the only option was to break open the cookie jar so he could get his hand out.

When she broke the jar, Tommy's mom was shocked to discover he was still clutching three cookies in his little hand. "Tommy, why didn't you *let go* of the cookies?!" she asked in amazement.

"But I *wanted* them!" Tommy replied as he broke into tears again.

If you find yourself stuck in a winter season today, you may need to let go of some "cookies" you've held on to. God wants to set you free from anything that has bound you and hindered your new beginning, but you need to *let go*.

COMPLETE SURRENDER

Like Tommy, you may be tempted to protest that the cookies you're grasping are something desirable and good—not something negative. But remember that *anything* is negative if it keeps us from God's best for our life. Paul says, *"**Whatever** things were gain to me, those things I have **counted as loss** for the sake of Christ"* (Philippians 3:7).

Today God offers you His "Get Out of Jail—Free" card, but you must let go of anything holding you back from your spiritual freedom in Jesus Christ. Once your surrender is complete, you'll be amazed by how quickly your new beginning comes into view and God gives you long-awaited breakthroughs through prayer.

> *Once your surrender is complete, you'll be amazed by how quickly your new beginning comes into view and God gives you long-awaited breakthroughs through prayer.*

So go ahead and thank God that since He has forgiven you, you are now able to forgive those who have caused you pain. Take time to go through the list of those who have hurt you, and forgive them, one-by-one, for what they did to cause you pain. As you do, repent for any anger, bitterness, or desire for revenge that may still be in your heart.

Today and in the days ahead, when the enemy tries to remind you of these past hurts, remind *him* that you have chosen to forgive these people as God has forgiven you, and that you are now set free in Jesus' name!

To be a Christian without prayer
is no more possible than to be alive
without breathing.

MARTIN LUTHER

15 STAND IN YOUR NEW IDENTITY IN CHRIST

This book was written with the assumption that you've already given your life to Jesus Christ and have an assurance of your forgiveness and salvation. However, it's important to take a few minutes to make sure this is true of your life.

The Bible says, *"If you confess with your mouth the Lord Jesus and believe in your heart that God raised Him from the dead, you will be saved"* (Romans 10:9). So when you confess and believe these truths, the Bible promises that you'll receive God's gift of eternal life. You'll have a home in Heaven with Him after you die, *and* you'll also receive the Covenant Blessings of His peace, presence, power, protection, and provision here on earth.

If you've never asked Jesus to be the Lord of your life, you can pray this simple prayer right now:

> *Dear Jesus,*
>
> *I need You. I confess that I'm a sinner and that You are holy. Jesus, I believe you are God's Son and that He raised You from the dead.*
>
> *Thank You for dying on the Cross for me and for providing the only way for me to have a relationship with God as my Heavenly Father. Please forgive me for all my sins, and wash me clean with Your blood. Come and live in my heart now, and fill me with Your Holy Spirit.*
>
> *Thank You for rescuing me and giving me the opportunity to live in Heaven with You forever. Please be the*

> *Lord of my life. Teach me how to love You and walk with You every day.*
>
> *I pray this in Your name. Amen.*

If you've prayed this prayer, you have been "born again" and saved by God's amazing grace. The angels in Heaven are rejoicing right now over *you!* Welcome to the family of God.

It's crucial that you understand who you are in Christ. Only then will you have boldness to claim God's promises and stand in His authority.

As we've encouraged you throughout this book, it's important for you to spend time with God every day. Talk to Him. Sit quietly and listen for the voice of His Holy Spirit to speak to you. And learn to be aware of His presence with you moment by moment.

As you grow and mature in your new faith and your knowledge of the Bible, you will learn to recognize the Lord's voice speaking to you in your mind and heart. He will bring you wonderful comfort and direction for your life as you gain a greater understanding of His Word.

The Lord has great things in store for you! Here is His promise:

> *I know the thoughts that I think toward you," says the LORD, "thoughts of peace and not of evil, to give you a future and a hope. Then you will call upon Me and go and pray to Me, and I will listen to you* (Jeremiah 29:11-12).

ALL THINGS BECOME NEW

If you have prayed to surrender your life to Christ as your Lord and Savior, God's Word declares many incredible truths about your new identity. No matter what you may have done before being born again in Christ, in Him you are a *"new creation,"* and Scripture says, *"Old things have passed away; behold, all things have become new"* (2 Corinthians 5:17).

In order to have an effective prayer life, it's crucial that you understand who you are in Christ. Only then will you have boldness to claim God's promises and stand in His authority.

We encourage you to take time to look up and meditate on these amazing verses about your new identity in Christ (1 Timothy 4:15). By faith, agree with what God's Word says about you, and claim His promises to you as His beloved child!

In Christ, you are...

- Justified, forgiven, and redeemed – Romans 3:24; Ephesians 1:7
- Crucified to your old, sinful self and raised to a new life – Romans 6:6; Ephesians 2:5; Colossians 3:1
- Free from condemnation – Romans 8:1
- Free from the law of sin and death – Romans 8:2
- Accepted by God – Ephesians 1:6
- Sanctified, holy, and set apart for God's purposes – 1 Corinthians 16:2
- Filled with wisdom, righteousness, sanctification, and redemption – 1 Corinthians 1:30
- Led in constant triumph – 2 Corinthians 2:14
- Liberated – Galatians 5:1
- Joined with other believers in God's family – Ephesians 2:11-22
- An heir of God – Galatians 4:7; Ephesians 1:11
- Blessed with every spiritual blessing – Ephesians 1:3

- Chosen, holy, and blameless before God – Ephesians 1:4
- Sealed with the Holy Spirit – Ephesians 1:13
- Seated in a Heavenly position – Ephesians 2:6
- God's workmanship, created for a life that bears good fruit – Ephesians 2:10; John 15:5
- Near to God – Ephesians 2:13
- A partaker of God's promises – Ephesians 3:6
- Bold and confident in approaching God – Ephesians 3:12
- Transferred from spiritual darkness into God's light – Ephesians 5:8
- A member of the Body of Christ – Ephesians 5:30
- Hidden with Christ in God – Colossians 3:3
- Guarded in your heart and mind by God's peace – Philippians 4:7
- Perfectly provided for, with all your needs supplied – Philippians 4:19
- Complete – Colossians 2:10

As you meditate on what God says about you in His Word, you will be *"transformed by the renewing of your mind"* (Romans 12:2). Satan's lies and accusations about you will be replaced by your new identity as *"the righteousness of God"* in Christ (2 Corinthians 5:21).

Remember God's great promise to those who meditate on His Word and receive it as true in their lives:

> *Blessed is the man who walks not in the counsel of the ungodly, nor stands in the path of sinners, nor sits in the seat of the scornful; but his delight is in the law of the LORD, and in His law he meditates day and night. He shall be like a tree planted by the rivers of water, that*

brings forth its fruit in its season, whose leaf also shall
not wither; and whatever he does shall prosper
(Psalm 1:1-3).

Be bold in claiming Biblical promises like this. As you delight in God's Word and walk in His ways, you will prosper and be blessed!

God does nothing
except in response to
believing prayer.

JOHN WESLEY

16 BELIEVE GOD FOR MIRACLES AND HEALING

There are many different kinds of healing and miracles. But whether your problem is physical, emotional, financial, or in a relationship, God can give you exactly the help you need.

Of course, God can and does use medical science to bring about healing in people's lives. I thank God for doctors and medicine and all that man can do to bring healing to those who are hurting.

It's important to realize the Lord can use an infinite number of "methods" to work His miracles. Once Jesus even healed a blind man by creating balls of mud to put in his eye sockets (John 9:1-7)!

SOME BIBLICAL EXAMPLES

If you or a loved one needs a healing today, take a look at some of these common ways the Lord healed people in the pages of Scripture:

1. The prayer of faith. James writes:

*Is anyone among you sick? Then he must call for the elders of the church and they are to pray over him, anointing him with oil in the name of the Lord; and **the prayer offered in faith will restore the one who is sick, and the Lord will raise him up,** and if he has committed sins, they will be forgiven him.*

Therefore, confess your sins to one another, and pray for one another so that you may be healed. The effective prayer of a righteous man can accomplish much (James 5:14-16).

There is great power in the prayers of God's believing people!

2. **Anointing with oil and laying on of hands.** James says the church leaders should pray over the sick person, *"anointing him with oil in the name of the Lord."* Likewise, Jesus' disciples *"were anointing with oil many sick people and healing them"* (Mark 6:13). And Jesus told His followers that *"they will lay hands on the sick, and they will recover"* (Mark 16:18). Oil is a picture of the Holy Spirit in Scripture, and the Lord instructs us to lay our hands on sick people to impact His healing touch.

3. **Repentance from sins.** The Bible makes it clear that not all sickness is the result of sin in a person's life (John 9:1-3), but it also indicates that sometimes sin is a factor. That's why James says of praying for the sick, *"...if he has committed sins, they will be forgiven him. Confess your sins to one another, and pray for one another so that you may be healed."* And after Jesus heals a sick man, He warns him, *"Behold, you have become well; do not sin anymore, so that nothing worse happens to you"* (John 5:14).

4. **Taking spiritual authority over the sickness or demon in Jesus' name.** Jesus speaks of those *"who will perform a miracle in My name"* (Mark 9:39). And Peter used the authority of Jesus' name to heal a lame man at the temple gate: *"In the name of Jesus Christ the Nazarene—walk!"* (Acts 3:6)

5. **Reading, listening to, and confessing God's Word.** Paul writes that *"faith comes by hearing, and hearing by the word of God"* (Romans 10:17). And the psalmist says, *"He sent His word and healed them"* (Psalm 107:20).

6. **Obedience.** Often God's promises for healing and other miracles are conditional, based on obedience to the voice of His Spirit or some principle in His Word. He says in Exodus 15:26:

   If you diligently heed the voice of the LORD your God and do *what is right in His sight, **give ear** to His commandments and **keep all His statutes,** I will put **none of the diseases** on you which I have brought on the Egyptians. For **I am the LORD who heals you.***

7. **Receiving Communion.** The Lord's Supper (Eucharist) is a beautiful picture of our Covenant Relationship with God, and healing is part of our inheritance in that Covenant. That's why Paul warns the Corinthians about the consequences of their worldly and divisive conduct as they partook of Communion: *"For this reason many are weak and sick among you, and many sleep"* (1 Corinthians 11:30). Instead of God's healing power being released during the Lord's Supper, the Corinthians were reaping His judgment.

8. **Using a "point of contact."** Sometimes people in the Bible used some object as a focal point to release their faith in God. For example, the woman who suffered with a hemorrhage proclaimed, *"If only I may **touch His clothes**, I shall be made well"* (Mark 5:29). And Acts describes powerful miracles through the apostle Paul: *"God worked unusual miracles by the hands of Paul, so that even **handkerchiefs** or **aprons** were brought from his body to the sick, and the **diseases left them** and the evil spirits went out of them"* (Acts 19:11-12). Was there some kind of magical power in the objects that these people used as a part of their healing? No, but these objects helped them focus their faith on God's awesome ability to do miracles in their lives.

Remember: The key to God's miracles is not a *formula,* but a *relationship.* Though His methods may vary, His character will not. *"I am the LORD, I do not change,"* He assures us (Malachi 3:6).

God not only heals us, but He describes Himself as our HEALER: *"I, the LORD, am your healer"* (Exodus 15:26). Your prayers can release His healing power, both in your life and the lives of your loved ones!

Pray, and let God worry.

MARTIN LUTHER

17 PRAY GOD'S BLESSINGS ON YOUR CHILDREN AND GRANDCHILDREN

In Paul's second letter to his spiritual son Timothy, we learn that it was the powerful faith of Timothy's mother and grandmother that helped prepare this young man for tremendous ministry (2 Timothy 1:5). So don't underestimate the impact *your* faith can have on *your* children and grandchildren!

Children and grandchildren can be one of our greatest sources of joy. And because we love them so much, we also may suffer greatly on their account.

It's especially difficult when our children choose to turn their backs on the Lord and walk away from what they know to be true and good and right. As parents or grandparents, we may experience intense pain from their poor choices, and sometimes our hearts may break with grief.

There will be times when we'll walk through painful, grief-filled seasons with our children—seasons when all we can do is cry out to God on their behalf. Thankfully, we can trust the Lord to draw our children to walk closely with Him and serve Him with their whole hearts. Yet there may be valleys we have to walk through before we see God answer our prayers and intervene in our children's lives.

I once heard a story about a rebellious young boy who was causing his mom a lot of trouble. She sent him to a Christian camp in hopes that he would meet the Lord there. God's Spirit was really moving during one of the fireside services, and the boy ran out into the woods because he was determined not to be touched by the Lord.

The boy yelled up at the heavens, "Why won't You just leave me alone?" and he heard a voice say from above, "Then tell your mother to leave *Me* alone."

Your children need to know they won't be able to escape from the Lord, because you're constantly banging on Heaven's door on their behalf. Your children may be straying from God's purposes at the moment, but sooner or later God will pierce their hearts. Persevere. Be persistent in your prayers. Your answer will come.

> *During difficult times with your children, or grandchildren there are important principles to remember as you pray God's Word over them.*

CLAIMING THE WORD

During difficult times with your children, or grandchildren there are important principles to remember as you pray God's Word over them. It's really so simple!

First, ask the Lord to lead you to Scriptures to pray over the specific situations of your children or grandchildren. Then in your quiet time, during a Sunday message, in a conversation with a close friend, or in some other way, the Holy Spirit will give you verses that you can turn into powerful prayers.

For example, one time when we were praying passionately for our son Ben, the Lord led us to Jeremiah 31:16-17:

> *"Refrain your voice from weeping, and your eyes from tears; for your work shall be rewarded," says the LORD, "and they shall come back from the land of the enemy."*

> *"There is hope in your future," says the LORD, "that your children shall come back to their own border."*

When we read these words, we cried for joy. We had spent so many hours interceding on Ben's behalf, weeping and broken over his situation. God used His Word to remind us that He had a specific plan for Ben, and we made these verses a prayer for our son by inserting his name:

> "Thank You, God, that our prayers will be rewarded and that Ben WILL return from the land of the enemy. Thank You that there is hope. In Jesus' name, we declare today that Ben WILL come again to the borders of our home and God's Kingdom!"

And soon after this, Ben returned to the Lord! As we aligned our prayers with specific promises from God's Word, the Holy Spirit moved powerfully on Ben's heart.

MORE SCRIPTURES TO CLAIM

There are many other great Scriptures you can use as prayers over your children or grandchildren:

> *"Yes, I have loved* [name] *with an everlasting love; therefore with lovingkindness I have drawn* [name]. *Again I will rebuild [name], and* [name] *shall be rebuilt"* (Jeremiah 31:3-4).

> *"But now, thus says the LORD, who created* [name], *and who formed* [name]: *'Fear not, for I have redeemed* [name]; *I have called* [name] *by name;* [he/she] *is Mine. When* [name] *passes through the waters, I will be with* [him/her]; *and through the rivers, they shall not overflow* [him/her]. *When* [name] *walks through the fire,* [he/she] *shall not be burned, nor shall the flame scorch* [him/her] *'"* (Isaiah 43:1-2).

"[Name] *is poor and needy; make haste to help* [him/ her], *O God! You are* [name's] *help and* [name's] *deliverer; O LORD, do not delay"* (Psalm 70:5).

These verses are just a sample! Ask the Lord to lead you to other specific Scriptures that He wants you to use as powerful prayers of intercession over your children and grandchildren.. Here are a few more of my favorites, categorized according to specific needs:

1. **Salvation.** Lord, I pray that my children and grandchildren will "obtain the salvation which is in Christ Jesus with eternal glory" (2 Timothy 2:10).

2. **Growth in grace.** May they "grow in the grace and knowledge of our Lord and Savior Jesus Christ" (2 Peter 3:18).

3. **Love for God's Word.** Help them grow to find Your Word "more precious than gold...and sweeter than honey" (Psalm 19:10).

4. **Biblical self-esteem.** Help them develop self-esteem rooted in a strong realization that they are "His workmanship, created in Christ Jesus for good works" (Ephesians 2:10).

5. **Purity.** May the cry of their heart be, "Create in me a clean heart, O God, and renew a steadfast spirit within me" (Psalm 51:10).

6. **Filled with the Holy Spirit.** May they be "filled with the Holy Spirit," experiencing both the gifts and the fruit of the Spirit in their lives (Ephesians 5:18, Galatians 5:22-23).

7. **Fulfilling God's will.** May the Lord continually work in them "both to will and to do for His good pleasure" (Philippians 2:13).

8. **Examples to others.** Make them an example to others "in word, in conduct, in love, in spirit, in faith, in purity" (1 Timothy 4:12).

9. **Impact.** May all my descendants be blessed and "mighty on earth" (Psalm 112:2).

10. **Generosity and eternal rewards.** Grant that they "be generous and willing to share and so lay up treasure for themselves as a firm foundation for the coming age" (1 Timothy 6:18-19).

MY PRAYER FOR YOUR KIDS AND GRANDKIDS

Be encouraged today to pray and believe God's Word over your loved ones. Pray, watch, and wait for the Lord to bring about His destiny for their lives, and you will not be disappointed.

And now I would like to pray an adaptation of Isaiah 44:2-4 over you, your children, and your grandchildren:

> *"Thus says the Lord who made you and your children and grandchildren, and who formed you from the womb, who will help you: Fear not, my precious friend, for God has chosen you. He will pour water on you who are thirsty, and floods on the dry ground; He will pour His Spirit on your descendants, and His blessing on your offspring: they will spring up among the grass like willows by the watercourses."*

In Jesus' name. Amen.

The church on its knees
would bring heaven upon the earth.

E.M. BOUNDS

18 SHAKE THE WORLD THROUGH PRAYER

Prayer not only can transform your personal life and the lives of your loved ones, but it can also transform your church, your community, your nation, and even other countries.

Early in the last century, a world-shaking revival broke out in a dilapidated church building at 312 Azusa Street in Los Angeles. Only a few hundred people could fit into the "Azusa Street Mission," but repercussions were felt around the world as the Holy Spirit touched lives and brought dramatic healings for nearly three years. What started as a prayer meeting attended by a handful of spiritually thirsty believers has grown into the fastest-growing segment of Christianity today—with an estimated 600 million adherents.

What brought about this remarkable move of the Holy Spirit? The human leadership of the revival was clearly unimpressive by worldly standards. One of the leaders mightily used by God was William J. Seymour, an uneducated preacher who grew up in poverty as the son of former slaves. Before entering the ministry, Seymour was a railroad porter and a waiter at several restaurants. Smallpox had left him blind in one eye.

Eye-witness accounts of the Azusa Street Revival say little about Seymour's preaching or leadership skills—for those attributes weren't the secret to his effectiveness. Here's how one Los Angeles newspaper described Seymour's role:

> Their preacher [Seymour] stays on his knees much of
> the time with his head hidden between the wooden
> milk crates. He doesn't talk very much, but at times

he can be heard shouting "Repent"—and he's supposed to be running the thing...

The breakthrough at Azusa Street clearly wasn't the result of great preaching, marketing techniques, financial backing, or organizational skills. Instead, the secret of the Azusa Street Revival was simply this: **world-shaking prayer.**

The very same power is available today—if we're willing to pay the price.

YOUR PRAYERS CAN SHAKE THE NATIONS

What does world-shaking prayer look like? In addition to the outpouring of the Holy Spirit at Pentecost (Acts 2), the early Christians experienced several other "power encounters" in response to their prayers:

> *When they had **prayed**, the place where they had gathered together was shaken, and they were all filled with the Holy Spirit and began to speak the word of God with **boldness** (Acts 4:31).*

While we might be awestruck at the physical shaking that occurred after these believers prayed, that was only a by-product of something much more important: They experienced a fresh encounter with God and new boldness to proclaim the Gospel. The church today needs this same kind of supernatural encounter with the Holy Spirit, but it will only happen as we give ourselves to passionate intercession, as the early believers did.

Sometimes our world-shaking prayers will arise from very difficult situations, as Paul and Silas experienced in the Philippian jail:

> *About midnight Paul and Silas were **praying** and **singing hymns of praise** to God...and suddenly there came a great **earthquake**, so that the **foundations***

*of the prison house were shaken; and immediately
all the doors were opened and everyone's chains were
unfastened* (Acts 16:25-27).

Paul and Silas weren't *trying* to cause an earthquake, but simply were focusing their hearts on prayer and worship. Yet the result was a mighty shaking—not only in the earthly realm but also in the unseen realm of the Spirit.

It's significant that *"doors were opened"* and *"chains were unfastened"* as a result of their prayers and praises. Do you need doors to open in your life or the lives of your loved ones? Are you, your children, or your grandchildren shackled by the enemy in some area of health, finances, relationships, or peace of mind? Then it's time for world-shaking prayer and worship!

AWAKE, ARISE, AND ASK

Too many believers still have a "Now I lay me down to sleep" prayer life. Instead of shaking the world through their powerful intercession, their prayers are more akin to spiritual tranquilizers.

It's time for God's people to arise from slumber and shine the light of the Gospel to the ends of the earth! The prophet Isaiah exhorts us:

*Arise, shine; for your light has come,
And the glory of the LORD has risen upon you.
For behold, darkness will cover the earth
And deep darkness the peoples;
But the LORD will rise upon you
And His glory will appear upon you* (Isaiah 60:1-2).

This is a great day to be alive! Do you realize that *half* of all the people who have ever lived are alive TODAY? Yes, the world is filled with *"deep darkness,"* but we have an incredible *opportunity* to pierce it with the light of Jesus Christ. Today, God has put powerful new technological tools in our hands that enable us to span the entire globe in milliseconds!

Yet let's never forget the lesson of Azusa Street: A world-shaking revival will only come when there has first been world-shaking prayer. An awesome worldwide harvest is ours for the asking, but God commands us to **ASK**: *"Ask of Me, and I will surely give the nations as your inheritance, and the very ends of the earth as Your possession"* (Psalm 2:8).

DESPERATE INTERCESSION

William J. Seymour and the fledgling band of Christians at Azusa Street didn't pray lukewarm, passionless, or unbelieving prayers. Their prayers arose from an intense burden for new intimacy with God…for a breakthrough of power from on high…and for SOULS. Instead of the polite but powerless prayers we so often hear today, these believers were *desperate* in their intercession—often groaning for hours before the throne of God.

We say we want God to move powerfully in our lives, but where are the prayer warriors today who will cry out as Isaiah did: *"Oh, that You would rend the heavens and come down!"* (Isaiah 64:1)? To shake the earth, we need prayers that will *"rend the heavens."* We need *breakthrough* prayers!

God's heart breaks over the condition of the Lost, and He wants our hearts to break as well. Look at the apostle Paul's anguish for the Jewish people who had not yet met Jesus as their Messiah:

> *I have great sorrow and unceasing grief in my heart. For I could wish that I myself were accursed, separated from Christ for the sake of my brethren, my kinsmen according to the flesh, who are Israelites…* (Romans 9:1-4).

Do *we* have this kind of heartache as we consider the lost Souls sitting in darkness in the nations of the world? Are our passionate prayers of intercession ascending to God? Do we regularly plant sacrificial financial seeds to send the light of the Gospel around the world?

FROM BARRENNESS TO ABUNDANCE

This kind of world-shaking prayer can bring you from spiritual barrenness to fruitfulness and abundance. God offers you a life of blessing and prosperity, but that will only happen as you *draw near* to Him and learn to abide in His presence (John 15:5).

If you find yourself in a place of barrenness today, we encourage you to cry out with the same passion Rachel exhibited when faced with her inability to bear children: *"Give me children, or else I die"* (Genesis 30:1).

Barrenness was no small issue for Rachel. Although her passionate cry for children may seem extreme to us, this is exactly the kind of zeal the Lord wants us to have for *spiritual* children—seeing Souls born into His Kingdom.

This was the cry of our hearts as Barbara and I founded Inspiration Ministries in 1990, and our constant prayer ever since has been "Use us to send the Gospel to the nations!" And although we've seen a great harvest of Souls from the media outreaches of Inspiration Ministries, it's still not enough. We know that the best is yet to come.

God is calling us to pray passionate, desperate prayers—asking Him to truly *"give us the nations."* The nations are waiting…the Lost are waiting…and, most importantly, *God* is waiting—waiting for us to arise in faith and obedience to rescue those who are perishing.

Can Barbara and I count on you to join us in this exciting journey to help fill the whole earth with the knowledge of the glory of Lord (Habakkuk 2:14)? Now is the time for world-shaking prayers and sacrificial financial seeds into the harvest fields of God's Kingdom. And who knows? Perhaps God will *"rend the heavens and come down,"* using us to spark a worldwide move of His Spirit that will rock the world!

111

Faith is to believe what you do not see;
the reward of faith
is to see what you believe.

AUGUSTINE OF HIPPO

19 STEP INTO YOUR BREAKTHROUGH

Often a breakthrough doesn't come in our lives until we're willing to obey God's instructions and take some sort of step of faith. Without faith it's impossible to please Him (Hebrews 11:6), but our faith can unlock His favor and provision in amazing ways.

Four men in 2 Kings 7:3-14 received a dramatic breakthrough from God, and we can learn a lot from their example. These men were in a truly desperate situation. They were lepers…they were outcasts… their city was under attack…and they were starving. It wasn't a pretty picture. Hope was nearly gone.

Finally, these lepers got an idea. "*Why should we sit here until we die?*" they asked each other (v. 3). They realized that if they just sat there and did nothing, they would surely die. So they decided to take the risky move of going to the camp of their enemies, the Arameans. "*If they spare us, we will live; and if they kill us, we will but die*" (v. 4).

To the shock of these four lepers, when they reached the camp of the Arameans, they discovered that the camp had been abandoned. Their step of faith—born of desperation—reaped an unbelievable harvest of silver, gold, clothes, and other bounty!

These men would surely have died if they had stayed at the outskirts of the city, grumbling, complaining, blaming others, and full of self-pity for their plight. But they took action—bold action—and received an incredible new beginning from God.

WHAT'S HOLDING YOU BACK?

Sometimes we're waiting on God to deliver us from some kind of difficult situation, when He's waiting on US to obey the voice of His Spirit and take action! As you pray for God's intervention in your circumstances, make sure you're also listening to His instructions on what you're to *do.*

The Bible is full of examples of people who received a breakthrough only *after* they took a step of faith: a geographical move…the sowing of a financial seed…an act of forgiveness and reconciliation…a season of prayer and fasting. Naaman had to dip seven times in the Jordan, the woman with the hemorrhage had to touch Jesus' cloak, and Job needed to pray for his friends.

Take a few minutes to examine your life in light of these Biblical examples of men and women who exercised their faith for God's breakthroughs, not allowing anything to hold them back:

- *If people or geography have held you back from your prophetic destiny in the Lord…*

  Remember **Abraham**, who at age 75 was called by God to leave his relatives and the idolatrous culture of Ur in order to venture out to a Promised Land that the Lord had prepared for him and his descendants (Genesis 12:1-4).

- *If you've been victimized and mistreated, causing you physical or emotional trauma…*

  Remember **Joseph**, who forgave his jealous brothers even though they had thrown him into a well and sold him into slavery (Genesis 50:18-21).

  Remember the **woman at the well** (John 4:1-42) and the **woman caught in adultery** (John 8:1-11), who both were traumatized at the hands of men and their own foolish choices—yet they each received a life-changing turnaround when Jesus forgave and restored them.

- *If you've been ridiculed, rejected, or labeled "a pain"...*

  Remember **Jabez**, who overcame a difficult childhood by crying out to God for a breakthrough of prosperity and blessing (1 Chronicles 4:9-10).

- *If you've suffered the grief and pain of losing a loved one...*

  Remember **Naomi** and **Ruth**, who found a wonderful new beginning when they moved back to Judah (Ruth 1:1-22).

- *If you've committed immorality or an act of violence against another person...*

  Remember **David**, who received God's forgiveness and cleansing after committing adultery with Bathsheba and murdering her husband, Uriah (Psalm 51, Psalm 32:1-5).

- *If you're facing insurmountable financial struggles...*

  Remember the widow at **Zarephath**, who found God's supernatural provision when she sacrificially provided for Elijah despite her own need (1 Kings 17:8-16).

- *If you're facing a serious illness...*

  Remember **Naaman**, the Syrian general who was healed of leprosy when he obeyed the prophet Elisha's instructions and dipped seven times in the Jordan River (2 Kings 5:1-27).

Remember **King Hezekiah**, whose life was extended by 15 years when he seemed to be on his deathbed (2 Kings 20:1-6).

Remember the **woman with a hemorrhage**, who suffered for 12 years before receiving a supernatural healing when she touched the hem of Jesus' garment (Mark 5:25-34).

- *If you've been bound by fear, depression, or some other form of oppression from the enemy...*

    Remember how Jesus set the **Gerasene demoniac** free from Satan's bondage into glorious liberty (Mark 5:1-20).

- *If you've allowed fear and cowardice to cause you to deny your relationship with the Lord...*

    Remember **Peter**, who denied the Lord three times yet received a new beginning of leadership in God's Kingdom (John 21:15-17).

- *If you've been religious, but realize you lack an intimate relationship with the Lord...*

    Remember **Nicodemus**, who learned that he needed to be born again (John 3:1-8).

    Remember **Saul of Tarsus,** who was zealous for religious laws, but was dramatically converted on the road to Damascus (Acts 9:1-19).

- *If you've strayed from God and squandered your life in wild living and addiction...*

    Remember the **Prodigal Son**, who experienced a turnaround and fresh favor when he made a decision to return to his father's house (Luke 15:11-32).

All these people—and many, many more—received breakthroughs from God when they believed Him and took steps to obey His instructions. They were just ordinary people who cried out to an extraordinary God.

Not only will God be faithful to give you a turnaround in your circumstances, but He will also be faithful to continue that work of transformation in the days, weeks, months, and years ahead.

As you are sensitive to the voice of God's Spirit, He will show you the steps of faith YOU need to take in order for your breakthrough to begin. Don't procrastinate. Don't make excuses or blame others for the difficult circumstances you face. And don't give up asking God for the breakthrough you need.

Remember: You have a Heavenly Father who loves you deeply. He has a fantastic plan for your life (Jeremiah 29:11). He wants to empower you with His Holy Spirit and give you every resource you need for an abundant life in Christ (John 10:10).

Not only will God be faithful to give you a turnaround in your circumstances, but He will also be faithful to *continue* that work of transformation in the days, weeks, months, and years ahead: Hold on to God's wonderful promise in Philippians 1:6:

He who began a good work in you will be faithful to complete it!

Resist your fear;
fear will never lead to you a
positive end.

Go for your faith and
what you believe.

T.D. JAKES

20 NEVER GIVE UP

The Bible teaches that perseverance is one of the most important ingredients for answered prayer. According to Hebrews 6:12, we inherit God's promises through *"faith and **patience"***—not faith alone!

In Luke 18:1-8, Jesus says we *"always ought to pray and not lose heart."* He goes on to tell the story of a woman who wouldn't stop pounding on the judge's door until she got a response, and that's exactly the posture we took when our children Ben and Becky seemed to be straying from God. We continually pounded on Heaven's door until we saw the fruit from our prayers manifested in their lives. We prayed and we prayed, and then we prayed some more.

Jesus promises us:

> *So I say to you, ask, and it will be given to you; seek,*
> *and you will find; knock, and it will be opened to you.*
> *For everyone who asks receives, and he who seeks, finds,*
> *and to him who knocks, it will be opened*
> (Luke 11:9-10).

The literal Greek translation of this passage says, *"Ask and **keep on** asking...seek and **keep on** seeking...knock and **keep on** knocking."* We must pray and keep on praying! We must never give up!

PRAYING WITH CONFIDENCE

This is true whenever we're seeking God's intervention in a troubling situation in our lives. Whether we are in need of a physical healing, a financial breakthrough, a new job, or a restored relationship, we must cry out to God with faith and tenacity.

Scripture tells us that Satan is like a restless, starving, roaring lion, pacing about and searching for victims to devour (1 Peter 5:8-9). He never stops prowling, so we must never stop praying. Our prayers are our greatest weapon as we wage war on behalf of our own destiny or our loved ones. And one of our most powerful prayer weapons is our ability to pray God's Word.

> *Ask and keep on asking... seeking...knocking...praying. Keep believing, keep trusting, and you WILL see God's goodness and faithfulness.*

This truth is so encouraging! What a joy to have confidence that when we pray the Word, God will do whatever we're asking Him to do.

Let's be honest. When our circumstances are desperate, it's easy to cling to our own opinions about what God should do. Yet God's ways are not our ways (Isaiah 55:8-9), so we don't always know what is best in a certain situation. Only He knows what must happen for peoples' hearts to change. This is why it's so important for us to pray Scriptures over our lives and loved ones.

REMEMBER GOD'S FAITHFULLNESS

When we experience difficult and painful times, there may be days when we struggle with doubt. But the Lord continuously reminds us that we are *His*. He loves us so much and is always carving out great testimonies from our experiences and challenges.

God asks us to trust Him with everything we hold dear, and sometimes He wants us to "back off" so He can move in our hearts and lives. We must choose to "let go" and place everything in His loving hands.

I encourage you to pray and totally surrender *every* concern to God. Ask Him to do whatever is needed to bring about His Kingdom in your situation.

Even when things seem to get worse before they get better, never forget that God and His mercies are new every morning (Lamentations 3:21-23). He loves you—and your loved ones—more than you can comprehend. You can trust Him 100% with your future...and theirs.

Never give up on the Lord as you ask Him to transform the difficult situations in your life. He is already at work, and He has a wonderful plan to bless you and your loved ones.

Ask and keep on asking...seeking...knocking...praying. Keep believing, keep trusting, and you *WILL* see God's goodness and faithfulness in your life and the lives of your loved ones.

This Scripture is our prayer for you today:

> *Wait on the LORD and be of good courage, and He*
> *shall strengthen your heart; wait, I say, on the LORD*
> (Psalm 27:14)!

Never give up on God, for He will never give up on you (Philippians 1:6)!

We are Here for You!

Helping to Change Your World Through Prayer

Do you need someone to pray with you about a financial need...a physical healing...an addiction...a broken relationship...or your spiritual growth with the Lord?

Our prayer ministers at the Inspiration Prayer Center are here for you. Because of God's goodness and faithfulness, His ears are attentive to the prayers made in this place (2 Chronicles 6:40).

"God does tremendous things as we pray for our Inspiration Partners over the phone. It's such a joy to see people reaching out to touch the Lord through prayer, and in return, to see God embrace them and meet their needs." – TERESA, Prayer Minister

Every day, Souls are being saved, miracles are taking place, and people are being impacted for God's eternal Kingdom! We continually receive amazing testimonies like these from people whose lives have been touched by our faithful prayer ministers:

Debt cancelled... *"After you prayed with me, I received the cancellation of a $23,000 medical bill. The hospital called it an act of charity, but I say it was God!"* – MELVIN, New York

Son found... *"I had not heard from my son for five years, but I miraculously found him just two weeks after your prayer minister called!"* – Z.C., Missouri

Cancer gone... *"Thank you for standing with me in prayer and agreeing with me for my healing. The Lord has healed me of breast cancer!"* – NORMA, Michigan

Family restored... *"Thanks so much for your prayers. I've got my family back! The Lord gave me a great job, my wife was willing to take me back, and I've been clean from drugs and alcohol for almost a year. God is so good to us!"* – L.B., Colorado

This could be YOUR day for a miracle! Let our anointed ministry staff intercede with God on your behalf, praying the Prayer of Agreement for the breakthrough you need.

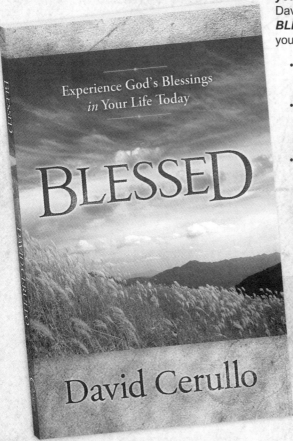